PAYING THE FARM BILL:
U.S. Agricultural Policy and the Transition to Sustainable Agriculture

Paul Faeth
Robert Repetto
Kim Kroll
Qi Dai
Glenn Helmers

WORLD RESOURCES INSTITUTE

March 1991

Kathleen Courrier
Publications Director

Brooks Clapp
Marketing Manager

Hyacinth Billings
Production Manager

T.L. Gettings/Rodale Press
Cover Photo

Each World Resources Institute Report represents a timely, scientific treatment of a subject of public concern. WRI takes responsibility for choosing the study topics and guaranteeing its authors and researchers freedom of inquiry. It also solicits and responds to the guidance of advisory panels and expert reviewers. Unless otherwise stated, however, all the interpretation and findings set forth in WRI publications are those of the authors.

Contents

Acknowledgments

We wish to thank those who provided assistance during the research and production process. Of particular note are Gary Lesoing, of the University of Nebraska's Research Station at Meade, who provided significant help in the interpretation and proper use of agronomic data for the Nebraska case study, and Verel Benson, of the Texas Agricultural Experiment Station at Temple, who provided invaluable aid in the use of the EPIC model.

Thanks are due to the many people who have reviewed earlier drafts of this research report including Kitty Reichelderfer, Pat O'Brien, Chuck Hassebrook, Sandra Batie, Ford Runge, Paul O'Connell, Mohamed El-Ashry, Bob Blake, Bob Livernash, Willy Cruz, Kathleen Courrier and Donna Wise. Special thanks go to Kathy Lynch, who edited the report, and Chuck Lee, who assisted at every stage of the project.

Finally, we owe thanks to Hyacinth Billings who managed the production process, and Karen Holmes who very ably assisted in the development of the project.

P.F.
R.R.
K.K.
Q.D.
G.H.

Foreword

In theory, U.S. agriculture is a business like any other, so depreciation of capital assets should show up in calculating net income. In practice, however, only man-made assets are treated this way. Farmers depreciate buildings and machinery, knowing that their future income will fall if they don't maintain or replace them. But they make no allowance for wear and tear when it comes to their most valuable assets—natural resources such as soil and water. Ruining natural assets costs money just as surely as new barns or tractors do, so ignoring resources is irrational. Farmers will pay in terms of lost productivity, but the larger cost to the environment will eventually be borne by the nation as a whole.

This agricultural blindspot is perpetuated by government policies and farm support programs that mask the negative effects of soil degradation on crop yields and incomes. The United States loses about 3 billion tons of its valuable topsoil from cropland every year despite the tens of billions of dollars it has spent on promoting soil conservation since establishing the Soil Conservation Service to deal with the Dust Bowl conditions of the 1930s.

Commodity programs that penalize resource-conserving rotation are causing farmers to jeopardize their future income by allowing soils to erode, groundwater to be contaminated, wildlife to be poisoned, and reservoirs to silt up. Yet, alternative farming systems that result in far less soil and chemical runoff are actually economically superior over much of America's farmland. To the extent that U.S. farmers, encouraged by perverse subsidies, are "living off their capital," their income is overstated today—and at risk tomorrow.

In *Paying the Farm Bill: U.S. Agricultural Policy and the Transition to Sustainable Agriculture,* a research team comprising Paul Faeth, associate in WRI's economic research program; Robert Repetto, program director; Kim Kroll, an agronomist with the Rodale Research Center; Qi Dai, a research associate in the Department of Agricultural Economics at Purdue University; and Glenn Helmers, professor of agricultural economics at the University of Nebraska, analyzes the changes needed to protect U.S. agricultural resources and income over the long term.

Paying the Farm Bill forges critical links that are missing in the current debate about sustainable agriculture, which is long on rhetoric, but short on policy analysis. The authors also rectify omissions in past comparisons of conventional and alternative farm practices, few of which compare farm profits under various policy scenarios and none of which compares the economics of conventional and alternative production systems when natural resources are accounted for. These are key omissions since any comparison that ignores natural resources will overlook the primary justification of sustainable agriculture.

This report's case studies contrast the results of several farming strategies in two places with very different kinds of land: Nebraska—where thick topsoil, flat topography, and sparse population limit damage from farm runoff—and Pennsylvania, where soils are shallow and farm runoff from the rolling hills drains into valuable lakes and estuaries. Implicit in the principal findings is a critique of current U.S. farm policy and practices:

• Where erosion-prone soils are causing substantial environmental damage both on and off the farm, resource-conserving production systems are economically superior. Even where soils are robust and environmental risks small, alternative farming methods can be financially and economically competitive.

• Current policy distorts comparative economics, inhibiting adoption of resource-conserving agricultural practices by making them less profitable. A system of farm income support that was not based on commodity support programs would remove distortions and make sustainable production systems competitive.

• Farmers who adopt resource-conserving production systems may suffer some short-term loss of income during the transition, but the long-term financial gains from maintaining or improving their land's productivity are substantial. The reverse is true with conventional farming methods. The greater the reliance on chemicals and the more disturbance through conventional tillage, the more damage to the soil. Falling productivity may be masked for a while by high-input production methods, but the economic loss is inevitable.

• Economic realities are obscured by traditional farm accounting systems, but the facts can be laid bare by environmentally honest accounting practices. In such a system, gross farm income is reduced by a soil depreciation allowance. The economic impacts of siltation on recreation and fisheries and of runoff on downstream water users are also factored in. Subsidy payments are excluded since they are not farm income but, rather, transfer payments from taxpayers to farmers. Under this system, where everything relevant counts, the traditional accounting method's $80-per-acre profit becomes a $26-per-acre loss.

This study's findings advance WRI's ongoing research on the economic changes that are required to make "sustainable development" a global reality, not just a slogan. Its policy recommendations complement and extend those spelled out in Dr. Repetto's recent studies, including *Wasting Assets: Natural Resources in the National Income Accounts* and *Promoting Environmentally Sound Economic Progress: What the North Can Do.*

WRI would like to thank The Joyce Foundation and the Wallace Genetic Foundation, Inc., for supporting the Nebraska and Pennsylvania case studies described in this report. The Ford Foundation and The Rockefeller Foundation have also provided essential support for our work on the economics of sustainable agriculture. To all these institutions, we express our deep appreciation.

Mohamed T. El-Ashry
Senior Vice President
World Resources Institute

WORLD RESOURCES INSTITUTE
PROJECT ON THE ECONOMICS OF SUSTAINABLE AGRICULTURE
ADVISORY PANEL

I. Overview, Policy Analysis and Conclusions

A. Introduction

For more than a half century, the U.S. government has used its many powers to support farmers' incomes. It has fixed prices, set floor prices, supplemented market prices, subsidized export sales, restricted competing imports, imposed limits on planting and marketing, insured farmers against production shortfalls, lent to farmers on favorable terms, and spent substantially from the public treasury on agricultural infrastructure, inputs, and research. Now, U.S. farm support programs use all these instruments.

The United States is by no means alone in this endeavor. Governments in Western Europe and Japan, whether socialist or conservative, have defended their farmers from market forces even more staunchly. Since each country's domestic farm policies affect its agricultural export supplies and import demands, usually to the detriment of competing foreign producers, conflicting agricultural policies create ceaseless international irritation and recrimination.

Farm programs have transferred income from consumers and taxpayers to farm producers, but at a heavy cost. Direct agricultural support payments in 1982–88 averaged 29 percent of farmers' incomes.[1] Their direct fiscal cost to U.S. taxpayers approximates $12 billion a year. Their total cost over the last five years was $93 billion (USDA, 1989). Higher prices and restricted supplies cost U.S. consumers between $5 billion and $10 billion a year in indirect or welfare costs (Carr et al., 1988; Bovard, 1989). The consumer- and taxpayer-costs of agricultural support in the world's industrial countries have been estimated at $150 billion annually (Carr et al., 1988).

Direct agricultural support payments in 1982–88 averaged 29 percent of farmers' incomes. Their direct fiscal cost to U.S. taxpayers approximates $12 billion a year. Their total cost over the last five years was $93 billion.

Most of these income transfers have not gone to the small, low-income farmers. Instead, because commodity support programs link benefits to the acreage historically under production, the largest benefits go to the largest producers. In 1988, the U.S. government's direct payments to farmers totalled about $14.5 billion. Nine billion of this went into the pockets of farm businesses while the rest went to those who own farmland and share-lease it to farmers. Forty-two percent of direct payments went to just 60,000 farmers who received an average payment of more than $75,000. These farmers had average net

1

cash incomes of almost $100,000 and net worths of nearly $750,000 (Schaffer and Whittaker, 1990). Clearly, small farmers are not the primary beneficiaries of these programs. Even though agricultural support programs are rationalized as protecting small farmers, agricultural production and land have become more concentrated, and the number of farmers has continued a long-term decline (National Research Council, 1989).

As agricultural support programs have grown increasingly complicated, so too has the web of restrictions and regulations governing what can be planted, how and where it can be grown, and who can grow it. Farming has become one of the country's most highly regulated industries. Cropping patterns and practices have changed, shifts in acreage have occurred among regions and crops, and input use and technology have become more intensive in response to these federal requirements (US GAO, 1990; National Research Council, 1989; Runge, Munson, Lotterman and Creason, 1990). Market interventions intended to transfer resources *to* agriculture have distorted the economic allocation of resources *within* agriculture.

Moreover, many farm policies are inconsistent. To boost production, for example, government subsidizes irrigation, extension services, research, and infrastructure—but simultaneously restricts cultivated acreage and pursues other policies to cut overproduction.

U.S. agricultural policies also carry with them serious unintended environmental costs. This is among the most pervasive and counterproductive of policy inconsistencies. Farm supports contribute to soil erosion, the overuse of agricultural chemicals, and the loss of wildlife habitat (Phipps and Reichelderfer, 1988; 1989). Policies that raise the payments farmers receive for their crops, but restrict the acreage they can plant, encourage intensive cropping and input use on the land that is planted (Phipps and Reichelderfer, 1988; National Research Council, 1989). Contamination of underground and surfacewaters by nitrates and pesticides has

emerged as a serious problem in many farming regions (Hallberg, 1989; Kahn, 1987; National Research Council, 1989), and a potential problem in many others (Nielsen and Lee, 1987).

Specifically, commodity programs have encouraged chemical-intensive monocultures, which deplete soil nutrients and pollute ground- and surfacewater. Farmers' eligibility for payments under commodity support programs is proportional to their established *acreage base*, the average amount of land planted in the preceding five years. Farmers are penalized for shifting acreage out of the supported crop because the acreage base (and government payments) are lowered over the following five years.

Deficiency payments are calculated for program crops as a product of the base acreage, the established yield, and the difference between the market price and the target price or loan rate, whichever is greater. When these deficiency payments rise as a percentage of the market price, as they have recently, farmers have strong incentives to maintain the highest possible base acreage. To take advantage of these incentives, farmers eliminate crop rotations that maintain soil fertility, control pests, and reduce erosion, and instead rely on chemical fertilizers and pesticides to maintain yields. In 1988, commodity support programs covered 90 percent of acreage planted to corn (Mercier, 1989), and 86 percent of acreage planted to wheat (Harwood and Young, 1989), so the disincentives to resource-conserving farming practices were extensive and powerful.

These disincentives are reinforced by other typical features of agricultural support programs. Until 1985, deficiency payments were based on historical yields as well as base acreage, which encouraged farmers to increase yields even after their marginal production costs exceeded the expected market price. Since then, though the yield base has been frozen, cross-compliance provisions further discourage rotations by effectively prohibiting farmers from shifting acreage from one program crop to another without sacrificing deficiency payments.

As U.S. agriculture has shifted from diversified crop-livestock farms toward large, specialized, input-intensive operations, soil erosion and chemical runoff have increased. Since 1964, agricultural pesticide use in the United States has tripled and fertilizer use has risen by two-thirds, but cropland has expanded by only 10 percent (Phipps and Reichelderfer, 1988). Rapid technological change and increasing input use have masked the productivity costs of soil erosion on the farm. Off the farm, agriculture has become the largest diffuse, or *nonpoint* source of water pollution (Smith et al., 1987; National Research Council, 1989). Annual damages to the rest of the economy from waterborne sediments exceed $10 billion a year, an estimated 36 percent of it from soil washed from croplands (Ribaudo, pers. comm., 7/10/90). Agriculture's share of these costs was equivalent to 10 percent of net income from farming in 1986.

These trends work against the nation's efforts to protect the environment and to conserve agricultural resources through programs such as the Soil Conservation Service and the Conservation Reserve Program. The Food Security Act of 1985 attempted to counteract these forces through conservation compliance regulations that denied commodity benefits to farmers who converted wetlands or highly erodible land to crop production. However, these provisions added another layer of regulation without altering the more fundamental incentives imbedded in the structure of agricultural policies.

The Food, Agriculture, Conservation, and Trade Act of 1990 (U.S. House of Representatives, 1990) went further in establishing environmental provisions than any previous Act,

Table 1. Annual Off-Site Damage from Soil Erosion

Damage Category	Best[b]	Range (U.S. $ Million)[a]	
Freshwater recreation	2,404	955 –	7,580
Marine recreation	692	497 –	2,772
Water storage	1,260	756 –	1,761
Navigation	866	616 –	1,078
Flooding	1,130	755 –	1,787
Roadside ditches	618	310 –	929
Irrigation ditches	136	68 –	184
Freshwater commercial fishing	69	61 –	96
Marine commercial fishing	451	443 –	612
Municipal water treatment	1,114	573 –	1,655
Municipal and industrial use	1,382	768 –	1,848
Steam power cooling	28	24 –	39
Total	**10,150**	**5,826 –**	**20,341**

Source: Ribaudo, 1989

a. Costs updated from 1986 to 1990 dollars using a multiplier of 1.157 derived from FAPRI, 1990b, p. 19.
b. Best estimate is the most likely extent of off-site damage.

adding provisions for an Integrated Farm Management Program Option, pesticide record-keeping and sustainable agriculture, and water quality research and education. The legislation also increased farm flexibility and market orientation by removing 15 percent of a farmer's base acreage from eligibility. Despite these improvements, the new legislation still maintains the distorting effect of commodity programs on most farmland.

U.S. agricultural policies and those of its trading partners could be redesigned to lower the fiscal, economic, and environmental costs of supporting farm incomes. Current agricultural policies in many countries distort commodity prices, and in so doing, drive a wedge between what is financially optimal to farmers and what is economically most valuable to society. Agricultural policy could be restructured to remove this distortion, so that farmers pursuing their own best interest would choose what is also better for society and the environment.

With this in mind, this report compares U.S. agricultural commodity support policies with alternative policy options. It is based on two case studies in locations at opposite extremes of environmental sensitivity, Pennsylvania and Nebraska. The Northeastern United States, including Pennsylvania, has the nation's highest environmental off-farm costs per ton of soil erosion because rivers drain into densely populated coastal areas where the economic value of water and water-related activities is high. The Northern Plains region, including Nebraska, has the lowest off-site erosion costs because the value of erosion impacts are low.[2] In Nebraska, on-site productivity losses associated with soil erosion are also lower because soils are deeper, less sloping, and therefore much less prone to erosion.

The framework developed for this study combines information from the field, farm, regional and national levels to provide an integrated analysis of the impacts of agricultural policy.

Table 2. Off-Site Damage per Ton of Soil Erosion, by Region

Region	Gross Erosion (t/yr) Millions	Off-Site Damage ($/t)[a] Best	Range	
Appalachian	486	1.63	1.48 –	2.61
Corn Belt	967	1.33	0.65 –	2.36
Delta	242	2.82	1.72 –	9.40
Lake States	181	4.32	2.30 –	6.92
Mountain	775	1.29	0.73 –	1.99
Northeast	187	**8.16**	4.85 –	16.25
Northern Plains	669	**0.66**	0.37 –	2.92
Pacific	679	2.87	1.76 –	5.49
Southeast	250	2.22	1.35 –	3.12
Southern Plains	490	2.33	1.33 –	4.50
Total	**4,926**	**2.06**	**1.19 –**	**4.13**

Source: Ribaudo, 1989

a. Costs updated from 1986 to 1990 dollars using a multiplier of 1.157 derived from FAPRI 1990b, p. 19.

(See Figure 1.) The analytical methodology, an extension of natural resource accounting, was designed to quantify economic, fiscal, and environmental costs and benefits of agricultural policy options. The methodology can be used to analyze the consequences of a wide range of policy interventions, used alone or in combination, including input subsidies, output price supplements, and acreage restrictions. Moreover, it can be used to analyze the environmental costs of farm policies both in physical and monetary terms, so that the benefits and costs of alternative policies can be compared. This methodology is a useful tool for analyzing farm policy options not only in the United States but in a wide variety of other settings as well.

The methods of natural resource accounting provide a relatively simple way to arrive at quantitative measures of sustainability. Soil productivity, farm profitability, regional environmental impacts, and government fiscal costs can all be included within the natural resource accounting framework.

The fundamental definition of income, the maximum consumption in the current period that does not reduce consumption in future periods, encompasses the notion of sustainability (Edwards and Bell, 1961; Hicks, 1946). Accounting systems for both businesses and nations have included a capital consumption allowance, which is subtracted from net revenues in calculating income, and represents the depreciation of capital during the current year. Historically, however, changes in productive capacity of the natural resource base, which, like other forms of capital provides a flow of economic benefits over time, have not been included in these accounts. Only changes in man-made capital are included in accounting systems, implying that the value of natural resource capital is of negligible value in current production systems. Nations, businesses, and farmers account for the depreciation of assets such as buildings and tractors as they wear out or become obsolete, but ignore changes in the productive capacity of natural resources such

as soil or water that result directly from the use of the resource, or indirectly from secondary impacts on the resource base from the production systems employed.

Thus, soil can be eroded, groundwater contaminated, wildlife poisoned, and reservoirs filled with sediment, all in order to support current agricultural practices and income. No depreciation allowance is currently applied against that income for the degradation of these assets, even though future income levels are jeopardized. Current accounting practices can mask a decline in wealth as an increase in income, i.e. "living off your capital."

For agriculture and other economic sectors that are fundamentally dependent upon the health of the natural resource base, the accounting of natural resource capital is extraordinarily important. When natural resources are not accounted for in farm, research or policy decisions, it should not be surprising that current agricultural production patterns may not be sustainable. In fact when changes in natural resource assets are ignored, resource degradation is encouraged, if not guaranteed.

This report rectifies key omissions in past comparisons of conventional and alternative practices. Few previous studies compare profitability under alternative policy scenarios, and none compare the economics of conventional and alternative production systems when natural resources are accounted for.[3]

These are critical omissions: if natural resource impacts are not compared, then the primary justification for sustainable agriculture will have been overlooked.

The core of the case studies reported here are economic comparisons between commonly used *conventional* farming systems, which rely on heavy inputs of fertilizers and pesticides, and *alternative* systems, which rely on crop rotations and tillage practices for soil fertility and moisture and pest management. These comparisons cover not only farmer's receipts

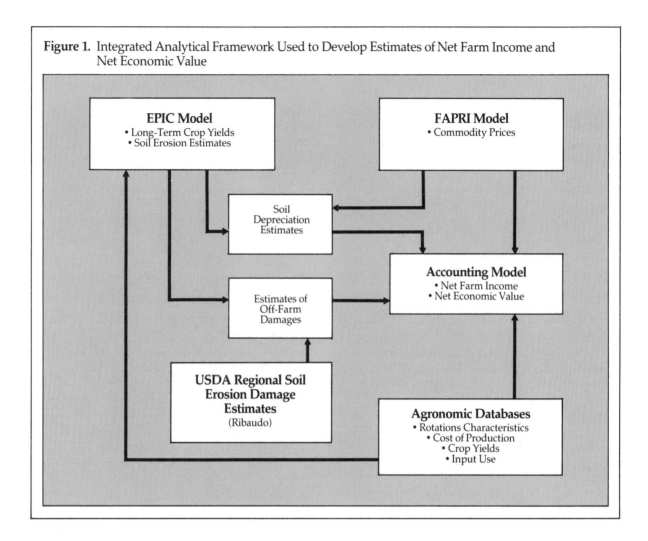

Figure 1. Integrated Analytical Framework Used to Develop Estimates of Net Farm Income and Net Economic Value

and production costs but also selected on- and off-farm resource and environmental costs.

Estimates of environmental costs are based on detailed physical, agronomic, and economic modeling of soil, water, and chemical transport from field into ground- and surfacewaters and the implications of these processes for water quality and soil fertility. Data from nine years of field experiments at the Rodale Research Center in Kutztown, Pennsylvania, and at the University of Nebraska at Mead were analyzed using the U.S. Department of Agriculture (USDA) Erosion-Productivity Impact Calculator (EPIC) Model (Williams et al., 1989). Output from this model was used to estimate the on-

and off-farm soil costs associated with conventional and alternative crop rotations. Other problems associated with agricultural production, such as groundwater contamination, loss of wildlife habitat, soil salinization or toxics build-up, and human health problems due to the use of toxics, though significant, were not addressed in this study. Hydrological models required for the examination of groundwater contamination issues, for example, are inadequate, so economic losses associated with groundwater quality cannot be determined.

Additionally, because of the nature of the case study approach, large-scale trade-offs in surface-water quality, soil erosion and groundwater quality could not be explored. Large benefits in one area may be offset by costs in another because of the possibility of widespread land use changes (Hrubovcak et al., 1990). Crutchfield (1988) has estimated changes in nitrogen in surface runoff and leachate for a variety of different soil conservation practices. Some of these results show that even though total nitrogen losses may be reduced, some practices can increase the percentage of nitrogen leached. For example, the establishment of a permanent vegetative cover reduces nitrogen in surface runoff by 90 percent, but increases nitrogen in leachate by 26 percent.

In both case studies, each policy option is modeled to represent its constraints on and incentives to farmers. For example, the implications of different cropping patterns on farmers' base acreage and government support payment receipts are built into each analysis. Both the financial and economic value of each policy option are analyzed. The *financial* value (Net Farm Income) of a production program to farmers takes into account current and future transfer receipts but ignores environmental costs borne by others. By contrast, the same program's *economic* value to society (Net Economic Value) includes environmental costs but ignores transfer payments. Because the most financially rewarding production system to farmers may not generate the greatest economic value, some policy options may induce significant economic losses.

Nationwide, responses by individual farmers to shifts in agricultural policy strongly influence aggregate supplies of crops and market prices. In turn, changes in market prices strongly influence farmers' production decisions. Commodity price projections from agricultural sectorwide econometric models developed by the Food and Agricultural Policy Research Institute (FAPRI) have been used here to estimate the market prices that each policy option would generate (FAPRI, 1988; 1990a). In turn, these predicted prices were used in the farm-level case studies. Geographically specific case studies were needed to analyze policy consequences because of regional differences in soils, weather, population densities and levels of economic activity that lead to different regional responses to the same national policies. In this way, by linking aggregative models of the effects of different national policies on farm prices to farm-level analyses of production decisions, both economic and environmental consequences could be predicted.

Baseline policy, as represented by the Food Security Act of 1985 (FSA), is the point of departure for both case studies. Under FSA commodity programs (for wheat, corn, oats, sorghum, rye, barley, cotton, and rice), participating farmers may receive deficiency payments on their base acreage enrolled in the program. *Base acreage* is defined as the average acreage planted to the commodity in the past five years. On this base acreage, less a mandatory set aside, deficiency payments per unit of output are based on historical yields, frozen in the FSA to 1981–85 average levels, excluding the highest and lowest. Then, deficiency payments per unit of production are calculated as the difference between the *target price* and the market price or the crop loan price, whichever is higher. Participating farmers are also prohibited from planting any program crop for which they have no base or planting acreage in excess of the established base.

An alternative to the FSA commodity support programs, and the economic baseline for both case studies, can be described as *multilateral decoupling* (MLDC). This policy scenario approximates the goals of the U.S. government in the Uruguay Round of trade negotiations among participating countries in the General Agreement on Tariffs and Trade (GATT) (Ambur, 1988). The scenario assumes that all major trading countries eliminate both import restrictions and export subsidies on agricultural products. It assumes further that government income support payments are made directly to targeted farmers in ways that do not depend on production levels or decisions, so that border prices in all countries are transmitted directly to domestic markets (FAPRI, 1988).

This alternative is a radical departure from the agricultural policies that industrial countries have followed since World War II. It represents the economic baseline because it eliminates the distortion of resource use in agriculture under government market interventions, and instead lets real cost advantages determine national and regional production patterns. Farmers' profit-maximizing choices of production methods are neither constrained by supply restrictions nor influenced by distorted price relationships. The prices that would emerge under this policy option permit the most accurate economic comparisons of competing production technologies.

Other policy options require less extensive modifications in the structure of the commodity programs to widen farmers' flexibility for making production decisions. One such option was introduced as a legislative proposal in 1989, H.R. 3552, the Sustainable Agriculture Adjustment Act of 1989 (SAAA) (U.S. House of Representatives, 1989) and passed in similar form as the Integrated Farm Management Program Option in the Food, Agriculture, Conservation, and Trade Act of 1990 (U.S. House of Representatives, 1990). Also known as the Jontz Bill, the proposal is designed to enable farmers to adopt "resource-conserving crop rotations" without sacrificing commodity support benefits.

Under this bill, resource-conserving crop rotations are defined as crop rotations that reduce erosion and chemical use by alternating plantings of "legumes, legume-grass mixtures, legume-small grain mixtures, and legume-grass-small grain mixtures" (not including barley or wheat for human consumption). For rotations that qualify:

1. The acreage set-aside requirement can be waived if production of supported crops is reduced over the rotation by an amount equal to historical yields on set–aside acreage.

2. Cross-compliance provisions are waived so that other program crops can be included in the rotations.

3. Acreage planted to resource-conserving crops is included in calculating base acreages so that participating farmers who adopt resource-conserving crop rotations are not penalized by reductions in base acreages and future deficiency payments.

While the SAAA option was intended to be available to a limited number of farmers, and in fact passed with a sign-up limit of 3 to 5 million acres over five years, we have tested the program as if it were available to all farmers.

Another policy option modeled in the case studies resembles the *Normal Crop Acreage* (NCA) proposal introduced by the Bush administration (USDA, 1990). This option, too, was designed to increase planting flexibility for participating farmers in government programs. In this proposal, *normal crop acreage* is defined as the sum of a farm's acreage bases for each program crop plus historical plantings of oil-seeds. Acreage reduction requirements and acreage eligibility limits in baseline policy still apply, except that any program crop or oil-seeds may be planted on acreage not set aside without a reduction in base acreage and deficiency payments. Resource-conserving crops, however, may be planted but not harvested unless the producer forgoes deficiency payments on the harvested acres (USDA, 1990).

A final policy option is designed to address the off-site environmental costs of farm production, a *25-percent tax on chemical inputs*, based on the "polluter pays" principle. Under this scenario, baseline policy remains intact but fertilizer and pesticide costs are 25 percent higher. Analytically, the question is whether farmers would be more likely to adopt alternative agricultural production technologies if forced to bear the environmental costs that conventional practices foist on others. (The principal features of these policy alternatives are summarized in Table 3.)

A resource-accounting framework is applied in this report to regional case studies in Penn-

Table 3. Principal Features of Policy Options Tested

Baseline Policy	Continuation of 1985 Food Security Act
Sustainable Agriculture Adjustment Act of 1989 (H.R. 3552) (SAAA)	Farmers using resource-conserving rotations allowed 100 percent planting flexibility, maintenance of crop base acreages, waiver of crop set-aside acreage, and payments on forage crops
Normal Crop Acreage	100 percent planting flexibility, but no deficiency payment for nonprogram crops if harvested
Input Tax of 25 Percent	25 percent tax applied to inorganic fertilizers and pesticides
Multilateral Decoupling	Elimination by U.S., EC, Japan, etc., of all commodity programs tied to production

sylvania and Nebraska. Both case studies compare the conventional and alternative agricultural production methods used for more than nine years when data on yields, production costs, chemical use, and changes in soil conditions were monitored in the field. These data were generated through cropping system research at the Rodale Research Center and at the University of Nebraska and were analyzed in collaboration with scientists at those institutions. Net farm income and net economic value generated under various rotations were estimated under farm programs as stipulated in the 1985 Food Security Act and under various alternative policies.

Rotations Compared, Pennsylvania and Nebraska

Pennsylvania—Five-Year Rotations

CC	Continuous conventional corn
CCBCB	Conventional corn-soybean rotation
ACG	Alternative cash grain, corn-barley/soybean-wheat/clover-corn-soybean
ACGF	Alternative cash grain with fodder production corn-soybean-wheat/clover-clover-corn silage
ALLHAY	Continuous alfalfa production

Nebraska—Four-Year Rotations

CC	Conventional continuous corn with herbicide and inorganic fertilizer use
HFCB	Conventional corn-soybean rotation with herbicide and inorganic fertilizer use
FOCB	Corn-soybean rotation with inorganic fertilizer use only
ORGCB	Corn-soybean rotation with no herbicide or inorganic fertilizer use, manure applied during the corn year
HFROT	Inorganic herbicides and fertilizer, corn-soybean-corn-oat/clover
FOROT	Inorganic fertilizer but no herbicides, corn-soybean-corn-oats/clover
ORGROT	Organic rotation with manure application, corn-soybean-corn-oats/clover

Estimating resource costs. Estimates of soil run-off in the Pennsylvania and Nebraska sites from the EPIC model were linked to USDA figures on water pollution damage costs per ton of soil erosion in each region. These damage-cost estimates include losses to fisheries, industries, recreation, and other water uses (Ribaudo, 1989).

Tables 4 and 5 show estimated soil erosion rates, off-farm erosion costs, and the value of soil productivity changes for each rotation in the Pennsylvania and Nebraska cases. The off-farm erosion costs for the rotations are weighted according to the set-aside requirements. If, for example, 10 percent of the land must be taken out of production, the set-aside land is presumed to be planted in hay, which has a much lower erosion rate, and the average erosion rate is weighted accordingly. (*See Appendix A* for an example of the method of calculation.)

In Pennsylvania, soils are shallow and sloping, and surfacewaters drain into densely populated eastern cities with high water demands. On- and off-site resource costs are high, and the difference in resource costs between conventional and alternative rotations significantly affects both economic and financial comparisons. Soil quality is such that two distinct production phases are evident in the field trials: 1. a four-year transition period, when organic rotations yield less than conventional yields following a switch from inorganic fertilizers and pesticides, and 2. a subsequent normal period, when the alternative yields equal or exceed the conventional yields.

B. Principal Findings

The study generated two sets of findings: one concerning production systems, the other concerning policy options.

Table 4. Rotation Characteristics, Pennsylvania, under Baseline Policy

Tillage/Rotation	Soil Erosion (t/ac/yr)	Off-Farm Erosion Cost[a] ($/ac/yr)	Soil Depreciation ($/ac/yr)
Conventional Tillage			
Continuous Corn	9.26	69	24.8
Corn–Beans	6.07	47	24.6
Alternative Cash Grain (ACG)	4.25	32	(2.8)[b]
ACG w/Fodder	3.29	26	(8.4)
All Hay	0.66	5	(4.8)
Reduced Tillage			
Continuous Corn	7.15	53	24.4
Corn–Beans	5.29	41	23.8
Alternative Cash Grain	3.49	27	(3.6)
ACG w/Fodder	2.49	20	(10.2)

a. Estimated using a damage cost of $8.16 per ton. *See* Appendix A for an explanation of how these costs were calculated.
b. Parentheses indicate *appreciation* in soil productivity.

Table 5. Rotation Characteristics, Nebraska, under Baseline Policy

Tillage/Rotation	Soil Erosion (t/ac/yr)	Off-Farm Erosion Cost ($/ac/yr)	Soil Depreciation ($/ac/yr)
Continuous Corn	6.5	4.0	7.8
Corn-Beans			
w/Herbicides & Fertilizer	3.7	2.3	3.0
w/Fertilizer only	3.7	2.3	2.8
w/Organic treatment	3.1	2.0	(2.0)
Corn-Beans-Corn-Oats/Clover			
w/Herbicides & Fertilizer	3.1	2.0	(1.3)
w/Fertilizer only	3.1	2.0	(1.0)
w/Organic treatment	2.2	1.5	(4.0)

In Pennsylvania, where on-farm and off-farm environmental costs are relatively high, organic farming rotations are clearly superior to conventional, chemical-intensive, corn and corn-soybean production—agronomically, environmentally, and economically.

Alternative Production Systems. In Pennsylvania, where on-farm and off-farm environmental costs are relatively high, organic farming rotations are clearly superior to conventional, chemical-intensive, corn and corn-soybean production—agronomically, environmentally, and economically. Resource-conserving practices cut production costs by 25 percent, eliminated inorganic fertilizer and pesticide use, reduced soil erosion by more than 50 percent, and increased yields after the transition from conventional systems had been completed. *(See Part II for details.)*

By reducing soil erosion and improving water retention, farmers using these practices would reduce off-site damages by more than $30 an acre. They would also forestall a 30-year income loss with a present worth of $124 an acre by building soil productivity by 2 percent and preventing a 17 percent decline in soil productivity. Consequently, when all resource costs associated with soil erosion are included, resource-conserving farming outperforms conventional approaches by almost a two-to-one margin in net economic value per acre. *(See Tables 26 and 27, and Figures 2 through 7.)*

In Nebraska, where on-farm and off-farm environmental costs are relatively low, alternatives to the predominant, high-input, corn-bean rotation were found to be environmentally superior and economically competitive. Three different treatments for the corn-soybean rotation differed in net farm income and net economic value by no more than $2 per acre per year. These treatments were a conventional treatment that relied on herbicides and inorganic nitrogen and phosphorous; a mixed treatment that used inorganic fertilizer but no herbicides; and an organic treatment that relied on biological means of fertility maintenance and pest control, without any agrichemicals. The underlying financial calculations excluded any premia for organically produced crops in the analysis of net farm income, although in today's marketplace some organically grown commodities command a 10–20 percent premium. The same output prices were used in both case studies for all crops and all treatments, because if organic methods were used widely enough, the premia could be expected to diminish or disappear altogether. If the current premia were included, however, the net farm income for the organic corn-bean treatment would be 21 percent greater than for the agrichemical treatments.

In Nebraska, where on-farm and off-farm environmental costs are relatively low, alternatives to the predominant, high-input, corn-bean rotation were found to be environmentally superior and economically competitive.

The organic corn-bean treatment was competitive financially and economically, and superior environmentally. It reduced soil erosion 20 percent compared to the chemical-intensive corn-bean rotation, and 50 percent compared to continuous corn. Total environmental costs associated with soil erosion were lower by $5 per acre per year.

While alternative treatments of the corn-bean rotation performed well in financial and economic terms, alternatives to that rotation did poorly. Compared to a conventional corn-soybean rotation, an organic corn-soybean-corn-oats/clover rotation cut soil erosion by 40 percent and eliminated chemical fertilizers and

pesticides. The resultant savings in on-farm and off-farm environmental costs associated with soil erosion amounted to 15 percent of the gross operating margin. Though respectable, these savings failed to offset a yield disadvantage of 13 percent for corn and 8 percent for soybeans relative to the best conventional rotation. Moreover, oats generate less revenue than soybeans, and are a poor substitute financially. All three treatments of the conventional corn-soybean rotation thus outperformed all three treatments of the four-year alternative rotation by an average of 31 percent in terms of net economic value per acre under baseline policy. *(See Figures 8, 9, and 10 and Table 28.)*

These findings suggest that resource-conserving production systems will be economically superior for many farmers wherever off-site environmental damages are substantial and soils are vulnerable to productivity loss through erosion. Even where soils are robust and environmental risks are minimal, alternative treatments, relying upon biological production methods, could be financially and economically competitive.

Policy Alternatives

In both case studies, a policy of multilateral decoupling produces the greatest net economic value of any of the policy alternatives considered. Moreover, most U.S. farmers would do well financially if these policies were adopted multilaterally. Opening markets and reducing supplies from high-cost producers would mean higher crop prices, and ending program constraints would let farmers reallocate their resources more efficiently. Net farm operating income before government commodity payments would be uniformly higher in both regions under multilateral decoupling, because market prices could be expected to increase and farmers would receive undistorted market signals. *(See Figures 4, 7 and 10.)* For the different rotations and treatments, net farm operating incomes improve by a wide range: 22 to 224 percent in Pennsylvania and 16 to 203 percent in Nebraska. This conveys the important policy and budgetary lesson that if agricultural subsidies were targeted and delivered in less distorting ways, the fiscal costs of farm income support programs could be drastically reduced.

If agricultural subsidies were targeted and delivered in less distorting ways, the fiscal costs of farm income support programs could be drastically reduced.

Tables 6 and 7 show how a move to multilateral decoupling increases net economic value. In both cases, multilateral decoupling results in a higher net economic value for all rotations and treatments. In Pennsylvania in particular, significantly higher net economic values could be obtained by a movement away from conventional, to alternative rotations. In the normal period the net economic values of the alternative rotations are more than double that for conventional corn-beans.

For Nebraska, multilateral decoupling produces higher net economic values for all rotations but the corn-beans rotations are economically superior.

In Pennsylvania, where resource costs are high, farmers who take a long view (ten years) and respond to market signals would find resource-conserving rotations much more profitable than other farming systems under every policy scenario we tested. In addition, net farm operating income for all rotations is significantly higher under multilateral decoupling than under the other policy scenarios. Consequently, government subsidies could be greatly reduced with no loss of farm income.

Tables 8 and 9 show the fiscal savings possible from a move to multilateral decoupling. The tables show the income support required to achieve parity with the most profitable

conventional rotation under baseline policy, the benchmark for comparisons. These calculations were done assuming conventional financial accounting, excluding soil depreciation allowances.

Table 8, for Pennsylvania, is broken out for the transition period, the full ten-year analysis, and the normal period alone. During the transition period, the conventional corn-beans rotation in Pennsylvania is within $4 over five years of the net farm income under baseline policy. Thus, only a $4 direct income support payment is necessary to achieve parity. Because of the reduced crop yields during the transition period, the alternative rotations require income support payments which are higher by $58 and $78 over five years than those for the benchmark.

However, during the normal period, when crop yields are roughly equal to the yields for conventional practices *(see Figures 12 and 14)*, no direct income support is required for the alternative cash grain rotation and only $42 for the alternative cash grain with fodder rotation. These result in savings of $152 and $110 over five years, relative to the benchmark. Under multilateral decoupling the corn-beans rotation also requires no payment for parity and even for continuous corn, payments are lower by $26 relative to corn-beans under baseline policy.

In Nebraska, the three treatments of the corn-beans rotation would require much lower levels of government support to achieve parity, while the continuous corn and four-year rotations would require higher levels of government support.

Taken together, these results clearly show that government costs can be reduced and the economic value of agricultural production to society can be greatly increased by removing the distorting effects of baseline policy and encouraging farmers to respond to market signals.

However, society may need to help farmers financially to get them through the transition

Table 6. Increase in Net Economic Value Possible From a Move to Multilateral Decoupling[a]

Pennsylvania
Net Economic Value (NEV) and Increase in Net Economic Value

	Conventional Tillage				Reduced Tillage			
	CC	CCBCB	ACG	ACGF	CC	CCBCB	ACG	ACGF
Transition Period ($/acre/5 years)								
Baseline NEV	(575)	(132)	(88)	5	(510)	(112)	(58)	41
MLDC NEV	(307)	19	10	55	(233)	40	43	92
Increase	**(175)**	**151**	**142**	**187**	**(101)**	**172**	**175**	**224**
Transition Plus Normal Period[b] ($/acre/10 years)								
Baseline NEV	(919)	(61)	208	345	(796)	(23)	264	413
MLDC NEV	(359)	251	438	466	(222)	290	500	536
Increase	**(298)**	**312**	**499**	**527**	**(161)**	**351**	**561**	**597**
Normal Period ($/acre/5 years)								
Baseline NEV	(344)	71	296	340	(286)	89	322	372
MLDC NEV	(52)	232	428	411	11	250	457	444
Increase	**(123)**	**161**	**357**	**340**	**(60)**	**179**	**386**	**373**

CC   – Conventional continuous corn
CCBCB – Conventional corn-beans
ACG   – Alternative Cash Grain—Organic corn-barley/soybean-wheat/clover-corn-soybeans
ACGF   – Alternative Cash Grain w/Fodder—Organic corn-beans-wheat/clover-clover-corn silage

MLDC – Multilateral Decoupling

a. Increases (or decreases) in Net Economic Value for each rotation are based on the most profitable conventional rotation—the corn-beans rotation (CCBCB)—under baseline policy. The table shows the result of a movement from CCBCB under baseline policy to the given rotation under multilateral decoupling.

$$(\text{MLDC NEV}_{\text{ROTATION}} - \text{Baseline NEV}_{\text{CCBCB}} = \text{Increase}_{\text{ROTATION}})$$

These calculations assume output prices as in Table 4 for Multilateral Decoupling.

b. Normal period values have been discounted.

Table 7. Increase in Net Economic Value Possible From a Move to Multilateral Decoupling[a]

Nebraska
Net Economic Value and Change in Net Economic Value
($/acre/4 years)

	CC	HFCB	FOCB	ORGCB	HFROT	FOROT	ORGROT
Baseline NEV	72	480	**483**	474	348	344	340
MLDC NEV	250	561	561	553	458	449	445
Increase	**(233)**	**78**	**78**	**70**	**(25)**	**(34)**	**(38)**

CC   – Conventional continuous corn
HFCB   – Conventional corn-beans, w/herbicides and fertilizer
FOCB   – Corn-beans w/fertilizer but no herbicides
ORGCB   – Organic corn-beans
HFROT   – Corn-beans-corn-oats/clover w/herbicides and fertilizer
FOROT   – Corn-beans-corn-oats/clover w/fertilizer but no herbicides
ORGROT – Organic corn-beans-corn-oats/clover

MLDC   – Multilateral Decoupling

a. Increases (or decreases) in Net Economic Value for each rotation are based on the most profitable conventional rotation—the fertilizer-only corn-beans rotation (FOCB)—under baseline policy. The table shows the result of a movement from FOCB under baseline policy to the given rotation under multilateral decoupling.

$$(\text{MLDC NEV}_{ROTATION} - \text{Baseline NEV}_{FOCB} = \text{Increase}_{ROTATION})$$

These calculations assume output prices as in Table 4 for Multilateral Decoupling.

period, but, this would be a wise investment. Tables 6 and 8, for example, show that a payment of just $12 per acre per year higher than that for the conventional corn-beans rotation under baseline policy, would in five years result in a fiscal savings of $30 per acre per year and an increase in net economic value of $72 per acre per year. These numbers make a compelling argument for a change in baseline policy.

By contrast, baseline policy offers the highest financial support per acre to farms using the high resource-cost rotations and heavy agrichemical input levels. Table 10 shows that in both Pennsylvania and Nebraska, under baseline policy, the continuous corn rotation draws the highest per acre deficiency payment, has the highest on- and off-farm resource cost, and has the highest use of fertilizers and pesticides; alternative rotations relying upon biological fertility and pest management have the lowest resource costs but receive much less government support.

Baseline policy is so biased in favor of resource-degrading practices that, despite their long-term economic inferiority, even in Pennsylvania, farmers unable or unwilling to look beyond the transition period would continue to plant conventional corn-soybean rotations. Because high government support payments make conventional practices most profitable for farmers in the short run, baseline farm policies block resource-conserving alternatives even in regions where they are much superior economically.

Table 8. Fiscal Savings Possible From a Move to Multilateral Decoupling[a]

Pennsylvania
Government Payments and Savings

	Conventional Tillage				Reduced Tillage			
	CC	CCBCB	ACG	ACGF	CC	CCBCB	ACG	ACGF
Transition Period ($/acre/5 years)								
Baseline Payment	293	**176**	182	123	293	176	182	123
MLDC Payment	178	4	234	254	193	17	237	258
Savings	(2)	172	(58)	(78)	(17)	159	(61)	(82)
Transition Plus Normal Period[b] ($/acre/10 years)								
Baseline Payment	547	**328**	315	192	547	328	315	192
MLDC Payment	304	4	234	296	332	17	237	303
Savings	24	324	94	32	(4)	311	91	25
Normal Period ($/acre/5 years)								
Baseline Payment	254	**152**	133	69	254	152	133	69
MLDC Payment	126	0	0	42	139	0	0	45
Savings	26	152	152	110	13	152	152	107

CC   – Conventional continuous corn
CCBCB – Conventional corn-beans
ACG   – Alternative Cash Grain—Organic corn-barley/soybean-wheat/clover-corn-soybean
ACGF   – Alternative Cash Grain w/Fodder—Organic corn-beans-wheat/clover-clover-corn
            silage

MLDC – Multilateral Decoupling

a. Calculations are based upon the direct income support required for each rotation to achieve parity with the most profitable conventional rotation—the corn-beans rotation (CCBCB)—under baseline policy and using conventional financial accounting.
         (Baseline Payment$_{CCBCB}$ − MLDC Payment$_{ROTATION}$ = Savings$_{ROTATION}$)
These calculations assume output prices as in Table 4 for Multilateral Decoupling.
b. Normal period values have been discounted.

Table 9. Fiscal Savings Possible From a Move to Multilateral Decoupling[a]

Nebraska
Government Payments and Savings
($/acre/4 years)

	CC	HFCB	FOCB	ORGCB	HFROT	FOROT	ORGROT
Baseline Payment	199	100	**100**	100	100	100	100
MLDC Payment	286	8	10	41	131	140	155
Savings	**(186)**	**92**	**90**	**59**	**(31)**	**(60)**	**(55)**

CC	– Conventional continuous corn
HFCB	– Conventional corn-beans, w/herbicides and fertilizer
FOCB	– Corn-beans w/fertilizer but no herbicides
ORGCB	– Organic corn-beans
HFROT	– Corn-beans-corn-oats/clover w/herbicides and fertilizer
FOROT	– Corn-beans-corn-oats/clover w/fertilizer but no herbicides
ORGROT	– Organic corn-beans-corn-oats/clover
MLDC	– Multilateral Decoupling

a. Calculations are based upon the direct income support required for each rotation to achieve parity with the most profitable conventional rotation—the fertilizer-only corn-beans rotation (FOCB)—under baseline policy and using conventional financial accounting.

$$\text{Baseline Payment}_{FOCB} - \text{MLDC Payment}_{ROTATION} = \text{Savings}_{ROTATION}$$

These conditions assume output prices as in Table 4 for Multilateral Decoupling.

Because high government support payments make conventional practices most profitable for farmers in the short run, baseline farm policies block resource-conserving alternatives even in regions where they are much superior economically.

As an interim policy modification, or perhaps as a means to see farmers through the transition period, provisions that increase farmers' planting flexibility without decreasing their support payments would greatly improve the net farm income from alternative rotations relative to conventional rotations. The Sustainable Agriculture Adjustment Act, for example, would remove the bias in baseline commodity programs toward intensive monocultures. This legislation is significant because it substantially improves the financial results of the alternative rotations during the transition period. This might induce farmers in Pennsylvania to switch to the ecologically and economically preferable alternative rotations. *(See Table 27 and Figures 5, 6 and 7.)*

In Nebraska, the four-year rotations, substituting a year of oats and clover for soybeans, also improve under SAAA to within 4 percent of the net farm income for the corn-beans rotations. Under baseline policy this gap is 23 per-

Table 10. Government Deficiency Payments, Resource Costs and Nitrogen Use

Rotation	Deficiency Payment ($/ac/yr)	Resource Costs[a] ($/ac/yr)	Nitrogen Use (lbs/ac/yr)
Nebraska			
Continuous Corn	50	12	85
Corn-Beans			
w/Herbicide & Fertilizer	25	5	38
w/Fertilizer only	25	5	38
w/Organic treatment	25	0	0
Corn-Beans-Corn-Oats/Clover			
w/Inorganic inputs	25	1	41
w/Fertilizer only	25	1	44
w/Organic treatment	25	(2)	0
Pennsylvania			
Continuous Corn	59	93	150
Corn-Beans	35	72	75
Corn-Barley/Beans-Wheat/			
Clover-Corn-Beans	36	29	0
Corn-Beans-Wheat/Clover-			
Clover-Corn Silage	25	17	0
Continuous Alfalfa	0	1	0

a. Both soil depreciation and off-farm costs are included. *See* Tables 4 and 5.

cent. The organic corn-soybean rotation does not qualify under SAAA. *(See Table 28 and Figures 8, 9 and 10.)*

The Normal Crop Acreage program was designed on similar principles but gives farmers less flexibility than SAAA. NCA doesn't alter the relative economics of various rotations in Pennsylvania or in Nebraska. Moreover, removing farmers' option to take land out of production depresses prices. NCA's limited flexibility precludes extensive rationalization of resource use in agriculture, and reduces economic value below that achievable under either of the two preceding policy options.

As might be expected, a 25 percent input tax significantly discourages chemical use within any cropping pattern. A 25 percent agrichemical tax reduces the profits of chemical-using rotations, in which agrichemicals account for 15 to 30 percent of total production costs, relative to biological fertility and pest management alternatives. In the Nebraskan corn-beans rotation, for example, the tax makes the herbicide and fertilizer-intensive corn-beans treatment the least profitable of the three corn-beans treatments and virtually equalizes returns between the organic and the fertilizer-only treatments. It would only take a 12 percent pesticide and fertilizer tax to equalize net farm income for the herbicide and fertilizer-intensive

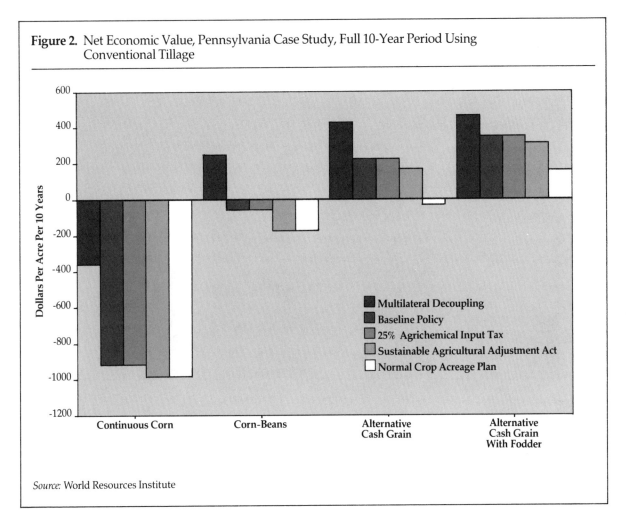

Figure 2. Net Economic Value, Pennsylvania Case Study, Full 10-Year Period Using Conventional Tillage

Dollars Per Acre Per 10 Years

■ Multilateral Decoupling
■ Baseline Policy
▨ 25% Agrichemical Input Tax
▨ Sustainable Agricultural Adjustment Act
□ Normal Crop Acreage Plan

Continuous Corn   Corn-Beans   Alternative Cash Grain   Alternative Cash Grain With Fodder

Source: World Resources Institute

corn-beans treatment and the organic corn-beans treatment, in Nebraska.

C. Conclusions and Recommendations

Even under the Food, Agriculture, Conservation, and Trade Act of 1990 (U.S. House of Representatives, 1990) the commodity programs that form the core of current agricultural policy, though somewhat reduced, remain basically intact. Despite provisions in the law requiring conservation compliance, farmers still have strong financial incentives to plant just a few crops and use energy-intensive chemical means of fertility maintenance and pest control.

Commodity programs (except the limited Integrated Farm Management Program Option) penalize farmers who diversify their cropping patterns. This discourages biological means of fertility maintenance and pest control. Only when commodity programs are restructured to give stronger financial incentives to economical, resource-conserving farming practices will American agriculture become sustainable.

Farm policy, as it now stands, induces farmers to ignore resource costs. Neither farmers nor taxpayers will benefit from this situation over the long haul. Farm policy should therefore be reconstructed to give all farmers financial incentives for conservation and wise resource use. The 1990 Act, while it moved in

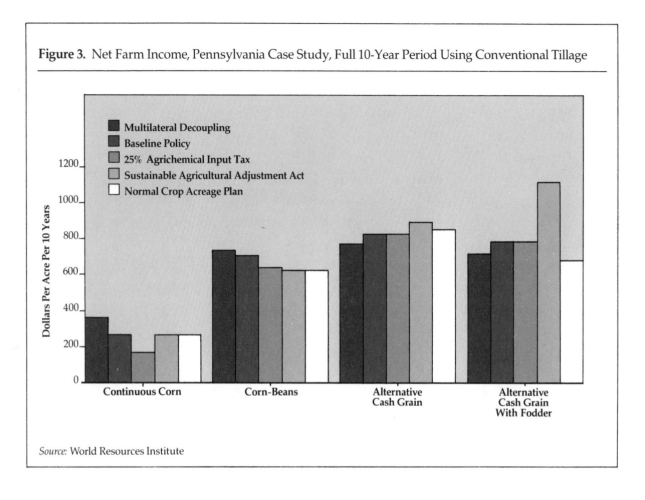

Figure 3. Net Farm Income, Pennsylvania Case Study, Full 10-Year Period Using Conventional Tillage

Legend:
- Multilateral Decoupling
- Baseline Policy
- 25% Agrichemical Input Tax
- Sustainable Agricultural Adjustment Act
- Normal Crop Acreage Plan

Y-axis: Dollars Per Acre Per 10 Years

X-axis categories: Continuous Corn, Corn-Beans, Alternative Cash Grain, Alternative Cash Grain With Fodder

Source: World Resources Institute

this direction, passed up opportunities to do this.

New policies can dramatically lower the resource costs of U.S. farming, while raising agricultural productivity and lowering the fiscal burden of supporting farm incomes. In one way or another, any successful policy will encourage farmers to recognize and cut resource costs by adopting alternative practices like those tested—and proven—in Pennsylvania and Nebraska.

Multilateral decoupling provides the greatest net economic value of the policies we tested. The simple fact that income support is not tied to commodity production allows market signals to reach farmers, encouraging them to use their resources in ways that are inherently

more efficient. In areas with high resource costs, farmers who take a long view would likely shift to resource-conserving rotations, while in regions with low resource costs, farmers would shift to less chemical-intensive practices.

The GATT negotiations now under way in Geneva provide an excellent opportunity to move toward this policy orientation in step with Europe and Japan, which also suffer heavy economic, fiscal, and ecological losses because of the present situation. Fortunately, the current U.S. administration has strongly adopted less distorted agricultural trade as a negotiating position. It deserves the support of American taxpayers, farmers, and environmentalists, who should recognize that they all would benefit if the U.S. negotiating position

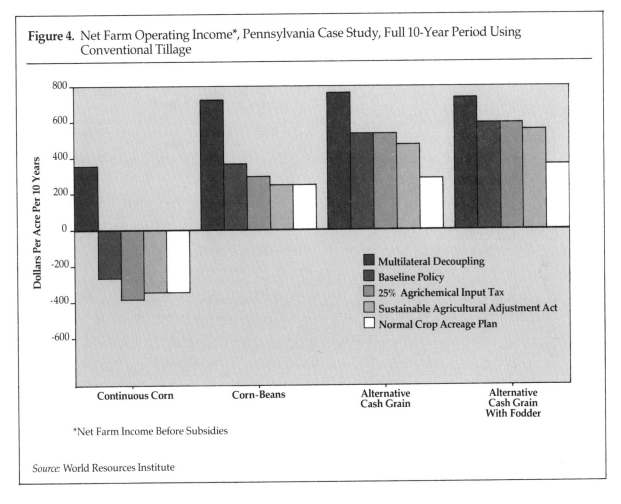

Figure 4. Net Farm Operating Income*, Pennsylvania Case Study, Full 10-Year Period Using Conventional Tillage

Dollars Per Acre Per 10 Years

- Multilateral Decoupling
- Baseline Policy
- 25% Agrichemical Input Tax
- Sustainable Agricultural Adjustment Act
- Normal Crop Acreage Plan

Continuous Corn   Corn-Beans   Alternative Cash Grain   Alternative Cash Grain With Fodder

*Net Farm Income Before Subsidies

Source: World Resources Institute

prevails. Environmentalists in particular should recognize that the answer to agriculture's environmental problems is not to tie on more regulations and cross-compliance provisions but to make the fundamental incentives farmers face consistent with the true values of the production systems available to them.

Unfortunately, because decoupling proposals have been associated with the elimination of farm income support, they have been highly unpopular among many farm groups. In reality, decoupling is an opportunity to increase the competitiveness of U.S. agriculture and its social value, to support income objectives directly in rural America, and to reduce environmental harm from farming. Previous rounds of GATT negotiations have stumbled

The answer to agriculture's environmental problems is not to tie on more regulations and cross-compliance provisions but to make the fundamental incentives farmers face consistent with the true values of the production systems available to them.

over agricultural protectionism as has the current round. Perhaps if it became clear that farm incomes could be protected at much lower fiscal

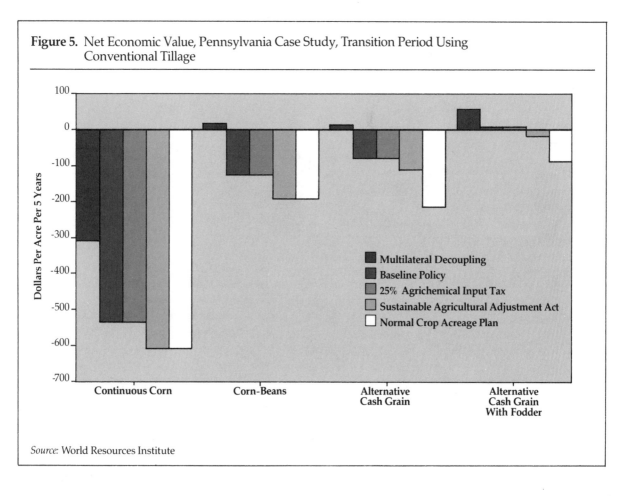

Figure 5. Net Economic Value, Pennsylvania Case Study, Transition Period Using Conventional Tillage

Dollars Per Acre Per 5 Years

■ Multilateral Decoupling
■ Baseline Policy
■ 25% Agrichemical Input Tax
□ Sustainable Agricultural Adjustment Act
□ Normal Crop Acreage Plan

Continuous Corn Corn-Beans Alternative Cash Grain Alternative Cash Grain With Fodder

Source: World Resources Institute

cost, that markets could be expanded, and that environmental damages could be reduced as well, it would be possible to achieve some common ground.

Farm income could be maintained at a lower fiscal cost by a movement to freer trade.

The United States government spends $12 billion every year on direct agricultural support, mainly through commodity programs. The analysis presented here suggests that farm income could be maintained at a lower fiscal cost by a movement to freer trade. Because of the current budget deficit, along with other reasons, these potential fiscal savings justify serious consideration of decoupling proposals. There could be significant savings, yet still enough money to restructure farm support away from convoluted commodity programs and into direct assistance to farmers and communities that most need it and whose resource management practices and environmental services warrant it.

This study also points to the need for significant reorientation in federally sponsored agricultural research programs. Not only has federally sponsored research into alternative farming methods been badly shortchanged, the criteria used to evaluate those methods in

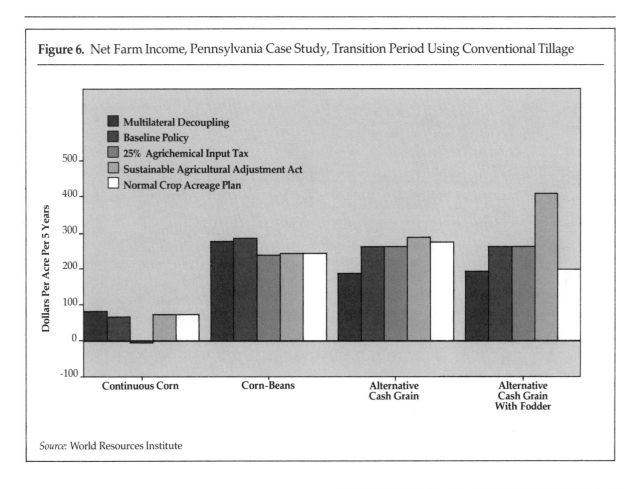

Figure 6. Net Farm Income, Pennsylvania Case Study, Transition Period Using Conventional Tillage

Legend:
- Multilateral Decoupling
- Baseline Policy
- 25% Agrichemical Input Tax
- Sustainable Agricultural Adjustment Act
- Normal Crop Acreage Plan

Y-axis: Dollars Per Acre Per 5 Years

X-axis categories: Continuous Corn, Corn-Beans, Alternative Cash Grain, Alternative Cash Grain With Fodder

Source: World Resources Institute

experimental and on-farm trials have also been seriously flawed by ignoring the value of impacts on natural resources. Both shortcomings should and can be remedied.

It would be reasonable to suppose that farming systems that drastically reduce off-farm pollution and on-farm soil degradation, while generating an economic return competitive with or superior to conventional methods, would receive a great deal of research attention. Not from private agribusiness, necessarily, since there is little return for private companies in improving technologies that *reduce* chemical use and production costs, but certainly from publicly funded research programs. However, that supposition would be erroneous, because only 2 percent of government agricultural research funds have been spent on alternative, low-input or organic farming systems (O'Connell,

Not only has federally sponsored research into alternative farming methods been badly shortchanged, the criteria used to evaluate those methods in experimental and on-farm trials have also been seriously flawed by ignoring the value of impacts on natural resources.

1990). Government research funds have supported and reinforced conventional farming systems, to the disadvantage of alternatives. This should change. A good start would be a

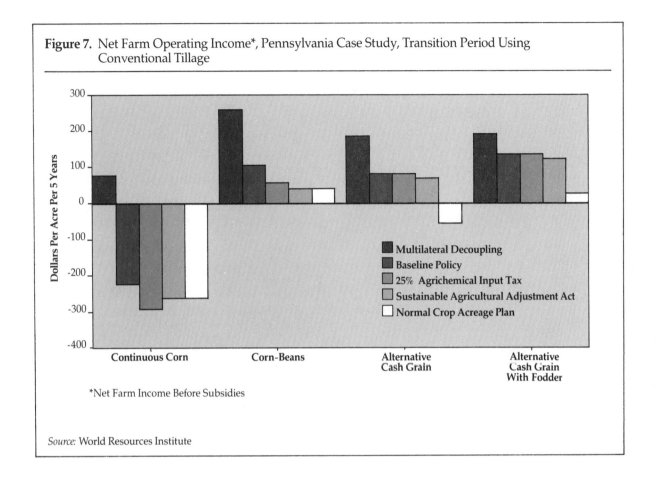

Figure 7. Net Farm Operating Income*, Pennsylvania Case Study, Transition Period Using Conventional Tillage

Dollars Per Acre Per 5 Years

- ■ Multilateral Decoupling
- ■ Baseline Policy
- ▨ 25% Agrichemical Input Tax
- ▨ Sustainable Agricultural Adjustment Act
- □ Normal Crop Acreage Plan

Continuous Corn   Corn-Beans   Alternative Cash Grain   Alternative Cash Grain With Fodder

*Net Farm Income Before Subsidies

Source: World Resources Institute

large increase in research support for Low-Input Sustainable Agriculture (LISA) systems.

Only 2 percent of government agricultural research funds have been spent on alternative, low-input or organic farming systems.

Another valuable immediate change would be for researchers throughout the government-funded agricultural research network to adopt criteria such as those used in this study to evaluate conventional and alternative production systems—criteria that account fully for on-farm and off-farm environmental costs, and that estimate the comparative returns to various systems free of the distorting effects of baseline agricultural policies. This study has demonstrated that faulty criteria and incomplete cost accounting can lead to erroneous conclusions about the relative value of conventional and alternative systems.

Of course, if the acreage restrictions and subsidies tied to production levels that are imbedded in the commodity programs were removed, the relative scarcity of agricultural production inputs would shift. Land would no longer be artificially scarce nor the returns to intensive farming artificially high. The financial and economic returns of alternative production systems would conform more closely.

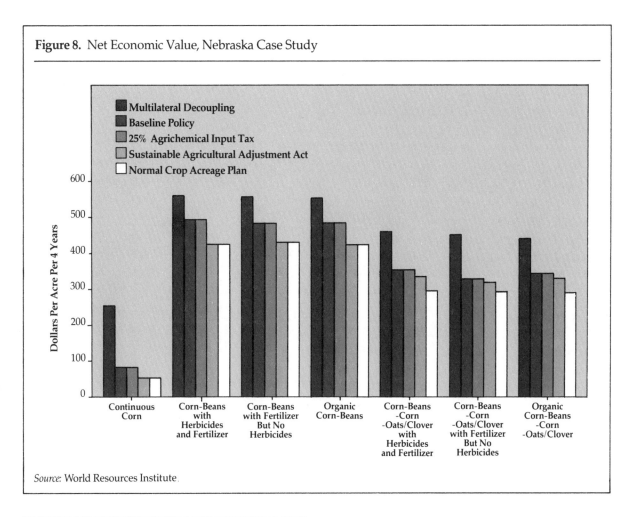

Figure 8. Net Economic Value, Nebraska Case Study

Legend:
- Multilateral Decoupling
- Baseline Policy
- 25% Agrichemical Input Tax
- Sustainable Agricultural Adjustment Act
- Normal Crop Acreage Plan

Y-axis: Dollars Per Acre Per 4 Years

X-axis categories:
- Continuous Corn
- Corn-Beans with Herbicides and Fertilizer
- Corn-Beans with Fertilizer But No Herbicides
- Organic Corn-Beans
- Corn-Beans -Corn -Oats/Clover with Herbicides and Fertilizer
- Corn-Beans -Corn -Oats/Clover with Fertilizer But No Herbicides
- Organic Corn-Beans -Corn -Oats/Clover

Source: World Resources Institute.

Faulty criteria and incomplete cost accounting can lead to erroneous conclusions about the relative value of conventional and alternative systems.

Additionally, agricultural production should not be exempt from the "polluter pays" principle. Incentives should be put in place that force producers to absorb the costs of the damages they cause. Given the flexibility of adjusted agricultural policy, and faced with the true costs of conventional farming practices, farmers would then demand, and researchers would develop, production methods that would most likely be less chemical-intensive (Runge, 1986; Hayami and Ruttan, 1985). Agriculture could come to rely more upon resource-conserving means of fertility and pest management and to recognize the value of natural assets. The catch in the "Catch-22" could be broken.

Agricultural production should not be exempt from the "polluter pays" principle.

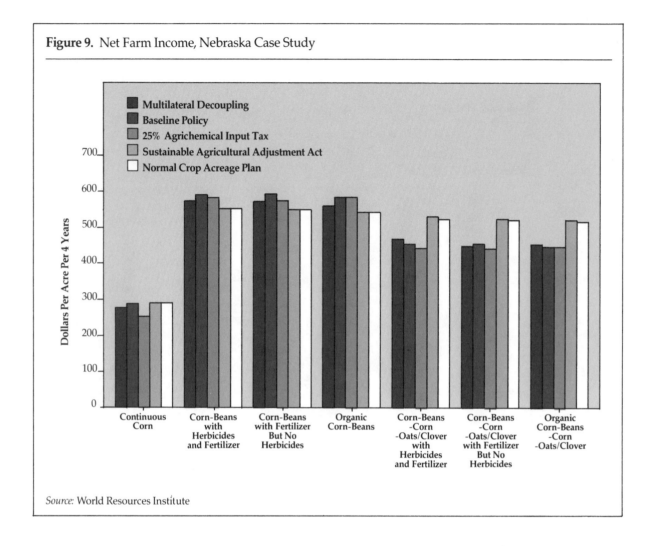

Figure 9. Net Farm Income, Nebraska Case Study

Dollars Per Acre Per 4 Years

- Multilateral Decoupling
- Baseline Policy
- 25% Agrichemical Input Tax
- Sustainable Agricultural Adjustment Act
- Normal Crop Acreage Plan

Continuous Corn

Corn-Beans with Herbicides and Fertilizer

Corn-Beans with Fertilizer But No Herbicides

Organic Corn-Beans

Corn-Beans -Corn -Oats/Clover with Herbicides and Fertilizer

Corn-Beans -Corn -Oats/Clover with Fertilizer But No Herbicides

Organic Corn-Beans -Corn -Oats/Clover

Source: World Resources Institute

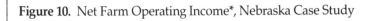

Figure 10. Net Farm Operating Income*, Nebraska Case Study

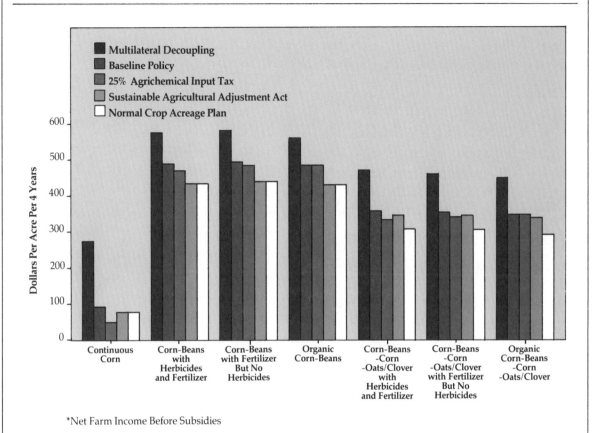

*Net Farm Income Before Subsidies

Source: World Resources Institute

II. Technical Summary and Supporting Data

The economic and resource accounting models used in this study integrate information from the field, farm, regional and national levels. They represent in a consistent framework the farmer's financial perspective and wider environmental and economic perspectives. Net farm income is the measure used to evaluate different production systems from the farmer's perspective. Net farm income is defined to include the value of changes in soil productivity, the farmer's principal natural asset. This definition is consistent with business and economic accounting practices, which incorporate asset formation and depreciation in their measures of income. Net farm income differs from net economic value, however. The latter is defined to take into account costs the farmers' activities impose on others, such as the costs of water pollution, but excludes transfer payments to the farmer such as subsidies and taxes.

This analysis uses models, or output from models, at four levels, corresponding to the four-fold hierarchy of sustainability defined by Lowrance (1986): field, farm, region, and nation.

A. Measuring Sustainability

At field level the USDA's Erosion-Productivity Impact Calculator (EPIC) model (Williams, et al., 1982) was used to simulate the physical changes in the soil that would occur under different agronomic practices and to generate estimates of soil erosion and productivity. EPIC, a comprehensive model developed to analyze the erosion-productivity problem, simulates erosion, plant growth, nutrient cycling, and related processes by modelling the underlying physical processes.

Net farm income differs from net economic value. The latter is defined to take into account costs the farmers' activities impose on others, such as the costs of water pollution, but excludes transfer payments to the farmer such as subsidies and taxes.

A simple farm-level programming model was developed for each case study to assess the impact of commodity programs—operating through changes in input and output prices, acreage constraints, and deficiency payments—on net farm income and net economic value. The EPIC and programming models were linked to calculate not only crop sales, production expenses, government deficiency payments and net farm incomes for each cropping pattern, but also soil erosion, off-site damages, and a soil depreciation allowance.

29

At farm level, estimates from EPIC of changes in soil productivity were used to calculate the economic depreciation of the soil resource. These estimates were combined with agronomic production data to determine the full on-farm production costs for each rotation and treatment. The farm level information on soil erosion was coupled with regional estimates of off-site damage per ton of eroded soil (Ribaudo, 1989) to derive estimates of off-farm damages resulting from each agronomic practice.

At the national level, agricultural sector models developed by the Food and Agricultural Policy Research Institute generated estimates of changes in crop prices under the various policies. (FAPRI, 1988; 1990a) These prices were then used in farm programming models to determine net farm income and net economic value. The farm-level models also generated estimates of government payments for the different crop production alternatives under the policy scenarios, which could then be generalized to compare the relative federal budgetary costs of different policy options. (See Figure 1.)

"The [FAPRI] commodity and policy analysis system consists of an integrated set of models used to provide quantitative evaluations of national and international policies, as well as other exogenous factors that affect U.S. and world agriculture. The objective of the system is to determine the consequences of alternative farm policy and program proposals for agricultural commodity markets and the U.S. agricultural sector." (Devadoss, et al., 1989)

The estimated market and target prices corresponding to each policy alternative are shown in Tables 11 and 12. Since no projections for the Sustainable Agricultural Adjustment Act of 1989 (SAAA) were available, prices corresponding to the Normal Crop Acreage

Table 11. Crop Prices—1992–96 Averages[a,b]

		Baseline Policy	Sust. Ag. Adjustment Act	Normal Crop Acreage	Multilateral Decoupling	25% Input Tax
Corn	($/bu)	2.05	1.97	1.97	2.53	2.05
Soybeans	($/bu)	5.80	5.24	5.24	5.26	5.80
Wheat	($/bu)	3.34	3.22	3.22	3.66	3.34
Barley	($/bu)	2.06	1.85	1.85	2.38	2.06
Oats	($/bu)	1.66	1.45	1.45	1.81	1.66
Alfalfa[c]	($/t)	85.00	85.00	85.00	85.00	85.00
Clover	($/t)	85.00	85.00	85.00	85.00	85.00
Corn Silage	($/t)	21.33	21.33	21.33	21.33	21.33

a. Crop prices come from FAPRI 1988 p. 42, and 1990a p. 35.
b. We have not included in this analysis a price differential between conventionally and organically grown products, even though a price differential does exist. Organically grown products can command a price up to 20 percent greater than that for conventionally grown products. (Ron Tammen, pers. comm., July 27, 1990).
c. Prices for alfalfa, clover and corn silage, are locally determined as these crops cannot be transported economically over long distances. As far as we could determine, there is no source for prices of these crops under the alternative policy scenarios. Rather than speculate on the impact of the policies on the crops, we used the average state prices for the 81–89 period.

Table 12. Target Prices[a] ($/bu)

	Baseline Policy	Sust. Ag. Adjustment Act	Normal Crop Acreage	Multilateral Decoupling	25% Input Tax
Corn	2.75	2.75	2.75	0.00	2.75
Wheat	4.00	0.00[b]	4.00	0.00	4.00
Barley	2.36	0.00	2.72	0.00	2.36
Oats	1.45	1.45	1.45	0.00	1.45

a. Target prices from FAPRI 1990a, p. 27.
b. For the alternative rotations we have assumed that the previous land use was continuous corn. Under the Sustainable Agriculture Adjustment Act, if there is no established base acreage for wheat or barley, no payments will be made unless the crop is interplanted with other small grains for non–human consumption. Therefore, the target prices for wheat and barley under SAAA for these particular alternative rotations are effectively zero and are presented here as such.

(NCA) option, the most similar, were adopted. Currently formulated as the Integrated Farm Management Program Option in the Food, Agriculture, Conservation, and Trade Act of 1990 (U.S. House of Representatives, 1990), farmer enrollment in this program is limited to 3 million to 5 million acres per year for a total of 15 million to 25 million acres. If made available to all farmers, different prices would emerge.

Under the NCA option, crop prices generally would fall because the 0-92 program, whereby farmers can plant zero percent of their acreage yet still receive 92 percent of their previous program payments, would be eliminated. If the 0-92 program were eliminated, some of the idled land would go back into corn, wheat, cotton, sorghum, and rice production, dominating the shift of acreage into soybeans, barley, and oats (FAPRI, 1990a).

The 25 percent input-tax scenario used the same prices as baseline policy projections. Moreover, throughout the study, market prices for organically grown commodities and for conventionally produced equivalents were assumed to be the same, although many organic farmers now get up to 20 percent

more. (Tammen, 1990) Ignoring this advantage biases the comparisons against organic production systems, but reflects the probability that as such systems were widely adopted and organically grown produce became more readily available, the price differential would narrow or disappear.

Prices estimated for the multilateral decoupling option increase for corn, wheat, barley, and oats, but decline for soybeans. Prices increase for the multilateral decoupling scenario because "[e]xport volumes exceed current levels by nearly 15 percent... This increase in demand for U.S. exports also drives up commodity prices, so that the value of exports increases by more than 15 percent. This increase in export value would be even greater were it not for the decline in soybean and soymeal prices that result from the reduced demand for soymeal from the EC." (FAPRI, 1988).

Analyses by other researchers also estimate general price increases under multilateral trade liberalization. Table 13 shows a summary of predicted world prices compiled by Blandford (1990). These studies suggest a general consensus that prices for wheat and coarse grains

31

Table 13. Comparison of Predicted Effects of Multilateral Liberalization on World Prices

Base Year	Wheat	Coarse Grains	Study (source)
		Percent Change	
1979–1981	−1	−3	OECD (1987)
1980–82	10	3	Tyers and Anderson (1987)
1984	7	11	USDA (Roningen & Dixit, 1987)
1985	2	1	Tyers and Anderson (1986)
1986	30	23	USDA (Roningen & Dixit, 1989)
1995	25	3	Tyers and Anderson (1987)
2000	18	11	Parikh and coauthors (1988)

Source: Blandford, 1990.

would increase under trade liberalization. These studies also uniformly predict price increases for rice, beef, dairy products and sugar (Blandford, 1990).

A natural resource accounting framework. Tables 14 and 15 compare net farm income and net economic value per acre for Pennsylvania's best conventional corn-soybean rotation, with and without natural resource accounting. Table 14, column 1, shows a conventional financial analysis of net farm income. The gross operating margin, crop sales less variable production costs, is shown in the first row ($45). Because conventional analyses make no allowance for natural resource depletion, the gross margin and net farm operating income are the same. Government subsidies ($35) are added to obtain net income ($80).

When natural resource accounts are included, the gross operating margin is reduced by a soil depreciation allowance ($25) to obtain net farm income ($20). *(See Table 14, column 2.)* The depreciation allowance is an estimate of the present value of future income losses due to the impact of crop production on soil quality. The same government payment is added to determine net farm income ($55).

Net economic value subtracts $47 as an adjustment for off-site environmental costs (such as sedimentation, impacts on recreation and fisheries, and impacts on downstream water users). Net economic value also includes the on-site soil depreciation allowance, but excludes income support payments. *(See Table 15 and Table 4.)* Farmers do not bear the off-site costs directly, but they are nonetheless real economic costs attributable to agricultural production and should be considered in calculating net economic value. Subsidy payments, by contrast, are a transfer from taxpayers to farmers, not income generated by agricultural production, and are therefore excluded from net economic value calculations. In this example, when these adjustments are made, an $80 profit under conventional financial accounting becomes a $27 loss under more complete economic accounting.

B. On-Farm Costs of Soil Depletion

Assessments of the influence of soil erosion on productivity have consistently concluded that erosion reduces soil productivity throughout the United States (Crosson, 1986; American Society of Agricultural Engineers, 1984; Pimentel,

Table 14. Conventional and Natural Resource Accounting Economic Frameworks Compared		
Net Farm Income ($/acre/year)		
	w/o Natural Resource Accounting	**w/Natural Resource Accounting**
Gross Operating Margin	45	45
– Soil Depreciation	–	25
Net Farm Operating Income	45	20
+ Government Commodity Subsidy	35	35
Net Farm Income	80	55

Table 15. Conventional and Natural Resource Accounting Economic Frameworks Compared		
Net Economic Value ($/acre/year)		
	w/o Natural Resource Accounting	**w/Natural Resource Accounting**
Gross Operating Margin	45	45
– Soil Depreciation	–	25
Net Farm Operating Income	45	20
– Off-site Costs	–	47
Net Economic Value	–	(27)

1987; Schertz et al. 1989; Heimlich, 1989; Alt, Osborn and Colacicco, 1989). Assessments differ, however, on the severity of these losses.

Many factors contribute to erosion's impact on soil productivity. The most serious loss is in the soil's capacity to hold water in ways plants can tap. In addition, crusting and other forms of degradation of the soil's surface structure induced by erosion restrict seedling emergence and root penetration. A third factor is the loss of such plant nutrients as nitrogen, phosphorus, and potassium, which can be dissolved in surface runoff or attached to soil particles that are moved during erosion (Frye, 1987; Larson et al., 1985).

Estimating Long-term Productivity Changes

In the field, erosion-induced productivity changes are almost impossible to isolate and measure accurately. Many other factors also affect crop yields, including weather, management, technology, and input use. Because there is no satisfactory methodology for separating the interacting effects of many factors on crop yields, soil productivity declines due to soil erosion can be easily masked.

For such reasons, in 1981 the USDA's Agricultural Research Service (ARS) organized a national erosion productivity modeling team, which developed a comprehensive tool, the EPIC model, to analyze erosion's effect on productivity. Based on representations of the physical processes of erosion, plant growth, nutrient cycling, and water movements in the soil, the model requires detailed soil and weather information as inputs. A comprehensive data base developed specifically for use with EPIC includes detailed soil data for 700 different soil series, and the average monthly weather data for 300 different locations in the United States. (Williams et al., 1989). EPIC can simulate the effects of crop rotations, tillage methods, soil conservation practices, and fertilizer use on crop yields, soil erosion rates, loss of soil nutrients, and many other soil factors. Output from the EPIC model includes crop yields, soil erosion rates, loss of soil nutrients in runoff and percolation, and changes in more than 30 variables that describe soil structure and properties.

Simulations of EPIC have been performed on 150 test sites in the continental United States and 13 sites in Hawaii. Simulated runoff and sediment were compared with actual measurements and the results were reported to be reasonably close (Williams and Renard, 1985). Crop yields obtained from the EPIC model were also compared with actual measurements for 12 research plots in 8 states. This model has produced reasonable estimates of crop yields under a variety of climatic conditions, soil characteristics, and management practices (Williams and Renard, 1985). However, before this study EPIC had not been tested with low-input rotations.

In this study, the EPIC model was used to estimate soil erosion and its impact on soil productivity for the conventional and alternative rotations in Nebraska and Pennsylvania. Estimated soil erosion rates for the different farming practices seemed reasonable, but simulated long-term soil productivity changes were not consistent with information from the field trials at the Pennsylvania site, for which calibration was first attempted.

Initial runs of the model overestimated observed yields for the conventional rotations by 10 percent or more, and underestimated yields of the alternative rotations by 8 percent or more. Initial runs predicted almost no decrease in productivity for conventional rotations, even after severe erosion and dramatic changes in soil structure and hydrology. Conversely, the model initially predicted no improvement in productivity for the alternative

rotations, although in the field trials yields improved considerably within a few years of transition away from agrichemical inputs.

In most runs of the EPIC model for the Pennsylvania site, estimates of soil bulk density increased over time. These estimates were not consistent with experimental results. In the low-input farming system trial at the Rodale Research Center, soil bulk density decreased nearly 20 percent from 1982 to 1986. At certain times of the year, the rate at which water infiltrated into the soil on the alternative plots was four times greater than on conventional plots. The soil-saturated conductivity, calculated from these bulk density estimates, also increased over time.

Erosion reduces productivity primarily through loss of the soil's capacity to make water available to plants (National Erosion-Soil Productivity Research Committee, 1981). The soil's water content is affected by many factors such as the maximum amount of water that the soil can hold, the density of the soil, and the ease with which water moves through the soil. In the EPIC model however, "soil saturated conductivity," a variable to which yield estimates are quite sensitive, is treated as a constant once calculated at the beginning of the simulation; changes in soil structure do not alter estimated saturated conductivity even as the soil erodes. Thus, the model omitted a key feedback from soil structure and organic content to soil productivity.

To overcome this difficulty, the simulation of the long-term soil productivity changes for different farming practices was accomplished in the following steps:

1. Parameters were set for the EPIC model using the appropriate soil series data from the EPIC database and measured field data;

2. The EPIC model was calibrated to bring the simulated crop yields in line with the measured crop yields;

34

3. The various crop rotations were simulated for the length of the crop rotation (five years for Pennsylvania, four years for Nebraska) without soil erosion. These estimates were taken to be the initial crop yields. Weather data for a normal year, that is without drought or excessive rainfall, was repeated for each year of the simulation.

4. The various crop rotations were simulated for 30 years with soil erosion and with a normal weather year repeated.

5. The value of some soil variables in the EPIC model (for example, the soil bulk density and the soil saturated conductivity) were replaced with values from the last year of the 30 year simulation, or with values based on data from the last year of the field trials where available.

6. The various crop rotations were again simulated for the length of the crop rotation without soil erosion, but with the recomputed values for several soil parameters. These estimates were taken to be the final crop yields.

As long-term soil productivity changes were simulated under unchanging weather and management conditions, the differences between the initial crop yields and the final crop yields were taken to be the result of long-term soil productivity changes.

Estimating a Soil Depreciation Allowance

Estimates of the long-term soil productivity changes taken from the EPIC model for different farming practices were then incorporated into present-value calculations to compute the economic impacts of soil productivity changes due to soil erosion.

The prices used to calculate the value of the productivity changes were those projected by the Food and Agricultural Policy Research Institute for each policy scenario tested. The yield change for each rotation period was taken to be the total yield change for the 30-year simulation divided by the number of rotations in 30 years, thereby assuming a linear change in yields. In this way the productivity change for each rotation included only the change attributable to that period. Since input costs were invariant to yields, this change in yields was then multiplied by the crop price to determine the loss in net farm income for the period. The present value of all income losses over 30 years into the future, using a 5-percent real (excluding inflation) discount rate, represents the loss in soil productivity. *(See Figure 11).*

The formula for determining the depreciation allowance is as follows:

Soil Depreciation Allowance =
$$[(Y_o - Y_n)/(n/RL)] * Pc * \{[1 - 1/(1+i)^n]/i\},$$
where Y_o is initial yield,
Y_n is final yield,
RL is rotation length,
n is period under consideration,
P_c is crop price, and
i is real interest rate.

For rotations that include more than one crop, each crop was weighted according to its acreage in the rotation, and these weighted crop depreciation allowances were added to determine the allowance for the rotation as a whole. When comparing rotations of different length, the rotation with the longest period was used to calculate the depreciation allowance for all rotations. *(See Appendix B for an example of these calculations.)*

The declining yields described by Figure 11 are not characteristic of U.S. agriculture in general.[4] In fact, the average yields for most crops in the United States have been rising, as new technologies have been adopted. Yet this does not mean that real economic losses have not occurred. Because the soil depreciation allowance measures soil productivity, not the productivity of the technology, the relevant issue is whether the technology is more productive on a better soil than on a degraded

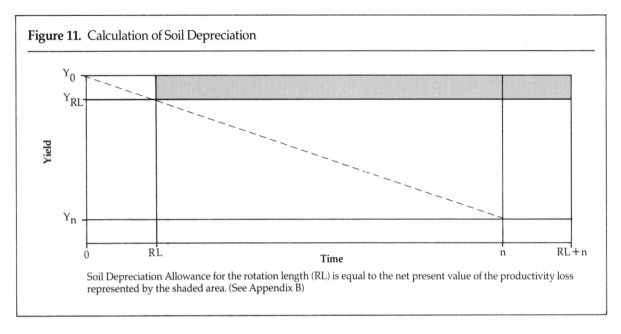

Figure 11. Calculation of Soil Depreciation

Soil Depreciation Allowance for the rotation length (RL) is equal to the net present value of the productivity loss represented by the shaded area. (See Appendix B)

soil. When technologies allow higher yields, some or all of the effect of soil degradation on yields may be masked by technological changes, even though the yield increases might have been greater had the soils not been degraded. This difference between actual and potential yield represents a real loss of income. A lower yielding technology or practice that does not damage the soil would have no concomitant soil depreciation. The yield trend in itself is thus irrelevant in calculating soil depreciation allowances; what matters is the difference between actual and potential yield. (See Walker and Young, 1986; Larson, Pierce, and Dowdy, 1983)

C. Off-Farm Costs of Soil Erosion

The off-farm costs of agricultural production due to erosion are also complex. Clark et al. (1985) estimated that annual off-farm damage from all sources of soil erosion was $8.1 billion, about $3.5 billion of it from eroding cropland.[5] Sediment washing off cropland and into waterways can fill reservoirs, block navigation channels, interfere with water conveyance systems, harm aquatic plant life, and degrade recreational resources. Agricultural pollutants include fertilizers, pesticides, and salts. If pesticides and nitrates in surface- and groundwater supply reach high enough concentrations, they can harm plant and animal life and endanger human health. Water quality degradation also damages recreational and commercial fishing, and water supplies for municipal and industrial use. (National Research Council, 1989)

Ribaudo (1989) of the Economic Research Service, USDA, has presented a comprehensive estimate of the off-site cost of soil erosion for different areas in the United States. *(See Tables 1 and 2)*. Off-site damages from soil erosion vary widely for different regions. In the Northeast, where many rivers drain into the densely populated seaboard and the economic value of water is high, damage per ton of erosion is $8.16 (1990 dollars). At the other extreme, in the sparsely populated, dry Northern Plains where the economic value of water is low, damage per ton of erosion is $0.66. These estimates were combined in this study with erosion estimates from EPIC to calculate off-farm resource costs for the various rotations. The erosion rates were weighted by the crop set-aside requirements, where applicable, and multiplied by the regional per ton damage estimates. These values are shown as the off-farm costs in Tables 4 and 5 and in Tables 26 through 28. (*See Appendix A.*)

D. Pennsylvania Case Study

The Pennsylvania case study[6] was based upon research conducted at the Rodale Research Center, which has accumulated an information base on the changes in plant dynamics, and on the physical and biological properties of soil during and after the change to alternative cropping systems. Beginning in 1981, the Farming System Experiment was established on a six-hectare tract of land in southeastern Pennsylvania on which corn had previously been grown using fertilizers, pesticides, and standard tillage practices.

The Rodale Research Center (RRC) is located in Berks County in southeastern Pennsylvania. Most of the county is characterized by rolling hills and a fairly uniform climate with an average annual precipitation of 42 inches. The soils—of shale, limestone, and gneiss origin—have been planted with a number of different field crops. The well-drained soils at the research site are formed from weathered shale and limestone, and range from shallow to deep in profile. The soils, formed from colluvium that have moved from the sides of the hills and have been deposited in the valleys, make up some of the most productive land.

Topography and soil types in southeastern Pennsylvania make the hill slopes highly susceptible to surface runoff, while the valleys are susceptible to leaching. This is Pennsylvania's most productive agricultural region, and has the largest number of farms. Hay, corn for grain and silage, and soybeans are normally the crops commanding the most acreage, in that order.

The RRC Farming System Experiment compares three representative farming systems:

1. A low-input animal system that represents a crop and livestock farm using manure prior to each corn crop and legume hay as nitrogen sources. This system uses a five-year crop rotation and produces corn, soybeans, small grains, and hay.

2. A low-input cash grain system that represents a farm with no animals needing a cash crop each year. The cropping system relies on diverse rotations and legumes for soil fertility and to produce cash grain crops.

3. A conventional corn and soybean system with purchased fertilizers and pesticides applied as recommended by Pennsylvania State University guidelines.

The research at the Rodale Research Center is one of few long-term experiments in the United States that compares soil biochemical changes and crop physiological changes under conventional and low-input farming systems. The experiments were designed so that statistical analysis could detect the results of different treatments. Information has been recorded for levels of macro- and micronutrients, acidity, cation-exchange capacity, and organic matter content, crop growth rates, crop yields, weather conditions, operation costs, material costs, and length of time for field operations. Although the soil is heterogeneous at the site, the field trials were designed to allow comparisons between systems. Weather conditions were identical for every farming system in the experiment, so the observed differences should be the result of different farming practices.

Alternative Practices and Yields

Five cropping systems based on the Rodale Farming Systems Experiment are included in this case study: 1. conventional corn-soybean (CCBCB); 2. alternative cash grain (ACG); and 3. alternative cash grain with fodder production (ACGF). Continuous corn and continuous alfalfa production systems have been included for comparative analysis. The data for 4. the continuous corn production (CC) are based on the two consecutive years of corn in CCBCB, and on previous similar studies by Penn State scientists (Crowder et al., 1984). The data for 5. continuous alfalfa production (ALLHAY) are obtained from the two consecutive years of hay in ACGF and the Kutztown Farm adjacent to the Rodale Research Center.

The rotations included here are summarized in the box.

improves crop yields is debated. Lower short-term, but greater long-term yields have been reported (Crosson, 1981).

Two different tillage methods are considered in this study: conventional tillage with mold-board plow; and reduced tillage with chisel plow. The conventional tillage method is used in the RRC Farming Systems Experiment. Data

---

Farming Systems Experiment, Rodale Research Center

1. Conventional Continuous Corn Rotation (CC)
   - *Rotation:* Five-year continuous corn production
   - *Weed control:* Penn State University (1987) herbicide recommendations
   - *Nitrogen fertility:* ammonium nitrate or urea based on Penn State University recommendations of 150 pounds per acre

2. Conventional Corn-Bean Rotation (CCBCB)
   - *Rotation:* five-year corn-soybean
   - *Weed control:* Penn State University herbicides recommendations
   - *Nitrogen fertility:* ammonium nitrate or urea based on Penn State University recommendations of 150 pounds per acre for corn

3. Alternative Cash Grain Rotation (ACG)
   - *Rotation:* corn-barley/soybean-wheat/clover-corn-soybean
   - *Weed control:* rotary hoe and cultivation for corn and soybean
   - *Nitrogen fertility:* legume green manure crops plowed down before corn

4. Alternative Cash Grain with Fodder Production Rotation (ACGF)
   - *Rotation:* corn-soybean-corn silage-wheat/clover-clover
   - *Weed control:* rotary hoe and cultivation for corn and soybean
   - *Nitrogen fertility:* animal manure applied before each corn and plowdown of hay

5. Continuous Alfalfa Production (ALLHAY)
   - No fertilizer or pesticides
   - Alfalfa hay cut three times per year

Tillage methods affect soil and chemical conservation very differently. Reduced tillage and no-till are usually described as ''conservation tillage.'' Conservation tillage saves topsoil and moisture and may also reduce water runoff because much of the residue from the previous crop stays on top of the soil. Conservation tillage, particularly no-till, also has some disadvantages. The protective layer of vegetation can harbor insect pests, plant diseases, and weeds and requires more pesticide use than other tillage systems. Crop yield responses to different tillage methods depend on soil, weather, and many other factors. Whether conservation tillage

for the reduced tillage are based on Penn State Agronomy Guide (1987) and on two previous studies in Pennsylvania (Crowder et al., 1984; Reid, 1985), which found no short-term interaction between crop yields and reduced tillage. Experiments at Penn State University by Beppler et al. (1981) achieved equal yields for all conventional, reduced-, and no-till methods. Yields for the reduced-till systems were therefore assumed to be the same as for conventional tillage. The long-term difference in resource costs associated with the reduced-tillage methods is, however, significant. *(See Table 4.)*

Table 16 presents actual crop yield averages for each type of crop rotation and tillage method in the transition and normal periods. *(See also Figures 12 and 13.)* Crop yields for the conventional corn-soybean rotation (CCBCB), alternative cash grain (ACG), alternative with fodder (ACGF), and continuous alfalfa (ALLHAY) were obtained from the Farming Systems Experiment. The continuous corn yield is assumed to be 10 percent less than that of the corn-soybean rotation. This assumption is based on a comparison of corn-after-corn and corn-after-soybean yields in the corn-bean rotation and previous empirical studies (Crowder et al., 1984).

Alternative farming systems often require a transition period to become fully established after a changeover from conventional farming (USDA, 1980). Crop yields often fall markedly during this transition and severe weed infestations may occur. Dabbert and Madden (1986) discussed three major reasons for this transitory effect: rotation adjustment, biological transition, and lack of experience with a different farming practice.

Before the Rodale Farming Systems Experiment began in 1981, this experimental plot grew corn with conventional farming practices and both fertilizer and pesticides. In the first five years of the Farming Systems Experiment, crop yields for corn in the alternative plots were lower than those in the conventional plots. In the second five years, however, corn yields in the alternative farming plot surpassed yields in the conventional farming plot. *(See Figure 12.)* Yields for wheat and barley, for which there are no conventional comparisons, also improved over the period. Results for

Table 16. Average Crop Yields from Rodale Experimental Trials

Transition Period							
Rotation	Corn (bu/ac)	Soybeans (bu/ac)	Wheat (bu/ac)	Barley (bu/ac)	Alfalfa (t/ac)	Clover[a] (t/ac)	Silage (t/ac)
Continuous Corn	97.10	—	—	—	—	—	—
Corn-Beans	106.80	42.76	—	—	—	—	—
Alternative Cash Grain	77.61	28.16	32.04	31.00	—	0.51	—
ACG w/Fodder	87.93	43.19	38.78	—	—	0.75	10.50
Continuous Alfalfa	—	—	—	—	1.25	—	—
Normal Period							
Rotation	Corn (bu/ac)	Soybeans (bu/ac)	Wheat (bu/ac)	Barley (bu/ac)	Alfalfa (t/ac)	Clover[a] (t/ac)	Silage (t/ac)
Continuous Corn	116.67	—	—	—	—	—	—
Corn-Beans	128.34	51.04	—	—	—	—	—
Alternative Cash Grain	130.31	45.13	34.40	31.00	—	0.90	—
ACG w/Fodder	129.53	43.36	45.15	—	—	1.75	16.19
Continuous Alfalfa	—	—	—	—	1.75	—	—

a. One half of clover harvested is for sale and another half is plowed down as green manure. Clover yield reported here only includes the half for sale and not the half for green manure.

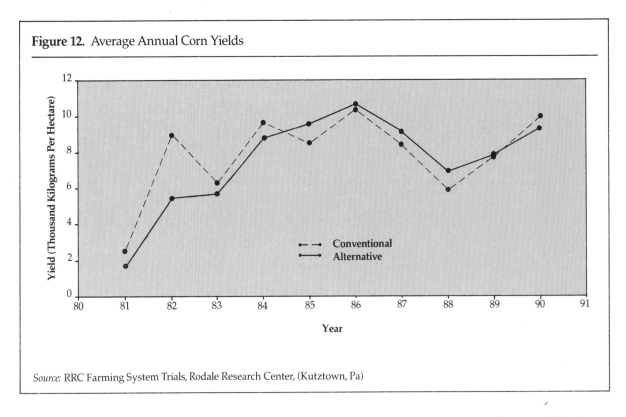

Figure 12. Average Annual Corn Yields

Yield (Thousand Kilograms Per Hectare)

- - - Conventional
——— Alternative

Year

Source: RRC Farming System Trials, Rodale Research Center, (Kutztown, Pa)

soybean yields are more mixed. *(See Figure 13.)* During the 10 years of the field trials, drought occurred in 1981, 1983, and 1988.

In the economic analysis, two periods, a transition and a normal period, are represented, each one encompassing a complete five-year rotation period. The first five years are considered the transitional period, the second five years the normal years. Since only nine years of data were available for a ten-year analysis, the fifth year of the experimental data was repeated at the end of the transition period and the beginning of the normal period.

The changes in soil properties over the first five years of the Farming Systems Experiments are shown in Table 17. Several notable changes can be seen, particularly in soil organic matter, soil acidity, cation-exchange capacity, and phosphorous content.

Table 18 shows the long-term yield estimates generated by the EPIC model for this case

study. EPIC estimated significant yield reductions for the conventional rotations, and small yield increases for the alternative rotations and for continuous alfalfa production.

Production Costs

Crop production costs in this study include operating costs, including those for machinery and material; labor; fertilizer and pesticides. All of these costs were normalized for the reference year 1990. Labor costs for field operations were included in the analysis but costs associated with management time were not. In the Farming Systems Experiment, fairly complete production cost data were recorded for each rotation.

Table 19 reports crop production cost data for each of nine production activities. Cost data for those activities with conventional tillage were obtained from experiment records. Cost data for reduced tillage were based on similar studies in Pennsylvania (Crowder et al., 1984;

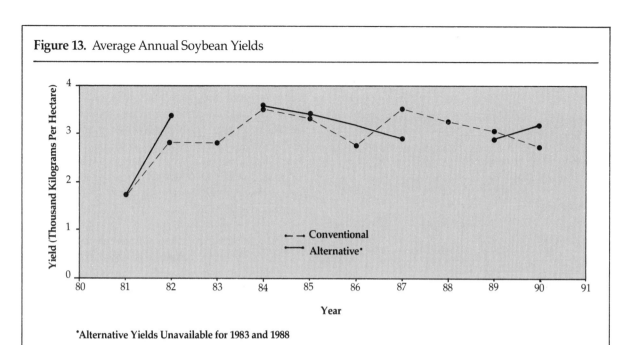

Figure 13. Average Annual Soybean Yields

*Alternative Yields Unavailable for 1983 and 1988

Source: RRC Farming System Trials, Rodale Research Center, (Kutztown, Pa)

Table 17. Soil Data from Rodale Research Center Field Trials

Year/rotation	pH	K	Mg	Ca	CEC[c]	P[a] (lb/ac)	OM[b] (%)
			Cations				
1981							
All systems bulked	6.7	0.56	1.4	7.6	11.8	323	2.4
1986							
Corn–Beans	7.0	0.21	2.1	7.2	10.4	317	2.4
Alternative Cash Grain	6.5	0.24	1.3	6.4	10.6	339	2.7
ACG w/Fodder	6.5	0.26	1.2	6.3	9.6	329	2.6

a. Phosphorous
b. Organic Matter
c. Cation-Exchange Capacity

Table 18. Yield Estimates for Pennsylvania Case Study Using the EPIC Model		
Rotation	**Yield** (bushels/acre)	
	initial	yr 30
Continuous Corn	136	113
Corn-Beans		
corn	141	121
soybeans	55.6	45.6
Alternative Cash Grain		
corn	135	137
soybeans	38.2	39.3
wheat	42.6	43.5
barley	38.1	39.3
clover (ton)	1.45	1.54
ACG w/Fodder		
corn	134	139
soybeans	40.9	42.2
wheat	48.3	49.2
clover (ton)	1.55	1.64
silage (ton)	18.5	19.5
Continuous Alfalfa		
(ton)	1.34	1.45

Dum et al., 1981). Fertilizer costs include both manufactured fertilizer and animal manure. The animal manure price used in the alternative cash grain with fodder system was based on the Kutztown Farm Report (Culik et al., 1983). The prices for production inputs were assumed to be the same for the different policy scenarios.[8]

Results of Policy Analysis for Pennsylvania

Within the accounting framework explained earlier, net economic values and net farm income are presented for a full ten-year period (two rotations) including a five-year transition period and a five-year normal period (*Figures 2,*

3 and 4; Tables 26A and 26B), and for the transition period alone *(Figures 5, 6 and 7; Tables 27A and 27B).* Because the normal period for the alternative rotations cannot be attained without going through the transition, it is irrelevant to show the normal period analysis by itself. In the ten-year analysis the returns for the normal period were discounted to the initial year.

The economic and financial results show a critical divergence, and both differ from incomplete, conventional accounting results:

- The net economic value generated by the best alternative rotation is higher than that of the best conventional rotation, not only under the decoupling policy option but under all policy options. This is true even in the transitional period when yields are depressed. During a ten-year period spanning both transitional and normal yields, alternative rotations produce almost twice the economic returns per acre. The large difference in on–farm and off-farm resource costs between conventional and alternative systems leads to this result.

- Nonetheless, under baseline policies and commodity support payments, farmers who could not or would not look beyond the five-year transitional period to the prospect of more normal yields thereafter would find conventional practices most profitable.

- Similarly, farmers who failed to factor long-term losses in soil productivity into their financial estimates would find conventional practices more profitable under all policy options except the Sustainable Agriculture Adjustment Act.

Policy options can be compared along with alternative farming systems. A policy scenario of multilateral decoupling of income support from agricultural production provides a useful benchmark for judging results under different policy scenarios because it minimizes the distortion of agricultural market incentives. No links are assumed between production and

Table 19. Production Costs and Crop Sales, Pennsylvania, under Baseline Policy
($/acre/10 years)

Tillage/Rotation	Total Production Costs	Operating Costs	Fertilizer & Pesticide Costs	Labor Costs	Crop Sales (Transition)	Crop Sales (Normal)
Conventional Tillage						
Continuous Corn	1004	590	260	154	896	1076
Corn–Soybean	861	534	179	148	1087	1302
Alternative Cash Grain	760	529	0	231	816	1248
ACG w/Fodder	796	561	0	235	887	1277
Continuous Alfalfa	477	271	0	206	531	701
Reduced Tillage						
Continuous Corn	1019	622	260	137	896	1076
Corn–Soybean	875	563	179	133	1087	1302
Alternative Cash Grain	758	550	0	208	816	1248
ACG w/Fodder	799	587	0	212	887	1277

income support—no supply control measures such as set-asides or base acreages, no import tariffs, no export enhancement, and no import quotas. Farmers would respond directly to market signals that were undistorted by agricultural policies. If these policies were adopted multilaterally, crop prices in the U.S. could be expected to increase as supplies from generally less efficient European and Japanese producers fell.

A policy of multilateral decoupling produces the greatest net economic value of all the policies tested. For the full ten-year period, the net economic value of the best alternative rotation is more than $466 an acre, the conventional corn-bean rotation is $251 an acre, and the continuous corn rotation is negative. If farmers shifted to alternative rotations, the gain in net economic value would be best measured as the difference between net economic value of conventional rotations under baseline policy and net economic value of the alternative rotations under multilateral decoupling—a difference as large as $1,385 per acre over ten years. Though financially profitable, conventional rotations lead to substantial economic losses under baseline

policies and modifications thereof, both in the transitional period and in the longer term.

Undistorted policies would simultaneously increase economic value and substantially reduce the costs of supporting farm income. Because crop prices would be higher under multilateral decoupling and because alternative rotations are intrinsically more profitable (see Figures 4 and 7), lower support payments would be needed to maintain farm income. Over ten years, for example, support payments for alternative rotations would average $23 per acre per year. By contrast, baseline support payments for the continuous corn rotation exceed $54 per acre per year. During the transition period, the best alternative rotation requires a payment greater than the best conventional rotation to achieve parity. Once the transition period ends and yields improve, no income support whatever is needed. This implies that the budgetary cost of support payments to maintain farm income in this region could be reduced by more than 50 percent, with much less environmental damage, under less distorted agricultural policies.

Baseline agricultural policy, by contrast, obscures the true economics of agricultural production systems. Policies intended to control supply and support income actually lower net economic value and net farm income in the long run, by favoring production systems with higher resource costs, discouraging adoption of resource-conserving methods, and raising on- and off-farm resource costs. The highest government support under baseline policy goes not to the rotations that produce the greatest net economic value but instead to the rotations with the lowest net economic value and the highest on-and off-farm resource costs. *(See Table 10.)* Baseline agricultural policy in this case is completely inconsistent with the underlying resource economics.

The distorting effect of the baseline policy is particularly evident during the transition period. Under baseline policy the conventional corn-bean rotation yields the highest net farm income, despite its much higher soil depreciation costs. *(See Figure 6 and Table 27B.)* Under baseline policy during the transition period, net farm income for the conventional corn-beans rotation is superior to both alternative rotations. Not surprisingly then, rotations that have high resource costs have become conventional. Under less distorted policies, with incentives provided that are in line with the underlying resource economics, resource-conserving rotations would become "conventional," not "alternative."

In order to sensitize farmers to the off-site resource costs of conventional practices, a tax on chemical inputs can be adopted as a modification of existing policies or other options. The 25 percent input tax, a transfer payment, does not change the relative net economic values of the rotations, *(see Figures 2 and 8)* but it does change net farm incomes. The net farm income of the alternative rotations, which are chemical-free, are improved relative to the net farm income of the conventional rotations. *(See Figures 3 and 6.)* During the transition period the 25 percent input tax is high enough to make both alternative rotations marginally

superior to the conventional corn-beans rotation; a 16 percent tax is enough to equalize net farm income for the conventional corn-beans and alternative cash grain rotation. In this case study, therefore, even grafted onto baseline policies, a 25 percent tax on chemical inputs would make farmers' financial incentives correspond to the basic economic ranking of production choices.

The shift in net farm income from conventional to alternative practices suggested by the levels of tax applied in these policy scenarios implies a much higher elasticity of demand (that is, a higher degree of substitution), for agrichemicals than has previously been reported (Council for Agricultural Science and Technology, 1980a; Daberkow and Reichelderfer, 1988; Hrubovcak, LeBlanc and Miranowski, 1990).

There are two possible reasons for this divergence. First, most elasticities of demand for agrichemicals are reported as short-term elasticities; the long-term price elasticities are uncertain. If agrichemical prices were increased and kept higher, farmers would search for, and researchers would develop, cheaper alternatives for pest and nutrient management, such as those detailed in this report. Over time, as substitutes were developed and proven, fewer agrichemicals might be used.

Secondly, price elasticities are developed using agricultural production functions. If these production functions do not include alternative treatments or management technologies, the elasticity of substitution will be underestimated. As alternative technologies have not been widely adopted yet, data used to estimate production functions will not have taken the potential substitutability of alternative practices fully into account. Different production function assumptions will result in different conclusions regarding the ultimate effect of an agrichemical tax (Hrubovcak, LeBlanc and Miranowski, 1990). The results presented here strongly suggest that the substitution possibilities for agrichemicals are greater than been previously considered.

Other modifications of baseline policies would have more far-reaching effects. Provisions of the Sustainable Agriculture Adjustment Act would affect net economic value and net farm income of various rotations through crop price adjustments (assumed similar to those under the Normal Crop Acreage program), as well as through transfer payments. The SAAA option would make net farm income under the alternative rotations more profitable than conventional rotations. The alternative cash grain system with fodder production has its highest net farm income for the ten-year period under SAAA. The impact of the SAAA policy alternative is most notable during the transition period, significantly improving the financial position of the alternative rotations during this critical time.

In terms of improving the profitability of alternative production systems, this legislative provision appears to work, but at a sacrifice of economic productivity compared to multilateral decoupling. Net economic value per acre is lower for each rotation under SAAA than for multilateral decoupling (or baseline policy) because of lower projected prices (recall that in the FAPRI projections the 0–92 program is assumed to be eliminated without the implementation of any compensating supply control). Compared to baseline policy, however, this option would induce farmers to switch away from rotations with high resource costs toward the more sustainable resource-conserving rotations, raising net economic value. If farmers switched from continuous corn production to alternative cash grain production with fodder, the gain in net economic value would be $1,234 per acre over ten years.

The normal crop acreage program has mixed impacts on net economic values and net farm incomes. Lower crop prices reduce net economic values of each rotation. The price of soybean, a crop not supported by target prices, drops, which also reduces the net farm income of the corn-beans rotation. Deficiency payments for program crops (mainly corn) expand to

cushion farm income. Compared to other policy options, this proposal is therefore economically and fiscally inefficient. Nonetheless, under this policy, alternative practices still appear clearly superior relative to conventional practices over the ten-year horizon.

Financially, the NCA program ban on the harvest of nonprogram crops if deficiency payments are received, hurts the alternative cash grain with fodder system, because the sale value of the fodder is too great to forego, even considering the loss of deficiency payments on those acres. Government payments for the alternative cash grain system without fodder are as high as those under continuous corn because a previous history of continuous corn production was assumed. Overall, this option is a costly and relatively ineffectual way of correcting farmers' incentives. This policy would do more to encourage agricultural sustainability if it were changed to accommodate both payments and sale of leguminous nonprogram crops such as clover and alfalfa, which are commonly used in low-input rotations.

In summary, the Pennsylvania case study shows that resource costs must be included in economic comparisons of alternative farming systems if valid conclusions are to be reached. It also shows the harmful economic, environmental, and fiscal effects of commodity support programs that distort farmers' incentives. Where on-site and off-site resource costs are high, resource-conserving production methods are not just feasible but more economical; to encourage widespread adoption of these methods, policy changes are essential.

E. Nebraska Case Study

The Nebraska case study is set in the dry east-central part of the State, where farms depend heavily on two crops, corn and soybeans.

East-central Nebraska lies at the western edge of the unirrigated corn belt, and on the eastern fringe of Great Plains agriculture to the west, where farms depend more than in the Corn Belt on winter wheat and cattle ranching. Nebraska has many irrigated farms in its central, northern, and western regions. About three-quarters of continuous corn production in the state is irrigated (Daberkow and Gill, 1989). Both gravity and center pivot irrigation systems are used to tap large groundwater reserves. Besides corn, farmers plant soybeans, winter wheat, grain sorghum, oats, and other crops.

Eastern Nebraska is a major cattle-feeding and hog-production area. In north central Nebraska, the Sandhills, a large grassland region, is well suited to cattle ranging. Permanent pastures are more common in the west of the state than in the east.

Trends in land use over the past thirty years in eastern Nebraska have paralleled developments elsewhere in the Corn Belt. Rotations involving oats and alfalfa have greatly diminished as fertilizer costs have declined, and the area of permanent pastures has shrunk (US GAO, 1990).

Continuous corn and corn-beans are the most common rotations used on land producing corn in Nebraska. On average across the state, 62 percent of the land planted to corn in 1988 was also planted to corn in the two preceding years; 22 percent was planted to corn followed by soybeans followed by corn. The continuous corn rotation is much more common in Nebraska than in other states of the Corn Belt. For the 10 major corn-producing states, 26 percent of land was in corn the previous two years, and 38 percent was in soybeans preceded by corn (Daberkow and Gill, 1989). Table 20 summarizes this data.

Environmental issues in agriculture have become important to most Nebraskans, non-farmers as well as farmers. Nitrate levels near or above the Environmental Protection Agency limit for drinking water (10 parts per million) have been documented in the water supplies of nearly one out of five rural communities, and a

number of them have had to modify their water systems as a result. Small amounts of the pesticide atrazine have also been found in water supplies in the intensively irrigated central Platte River Valley (Aiken, 1990).

Soil erosion is another concern, particularly in eastern Nebraska, where conservation compliance requirements have had to be enforced to protect the land. The shallow-rooted soybean crops are especially vulnerable to erosion. Minimum and no-tillage systems have been successful in Nebraska because they reduce water runoff, although they often require increased use of herbicides or a change in crop rotations.

Cropping Systems and Yields

Three basic cropping rotations were included in this analysis. These include corn-soybean (CB), continuous corn (CC), and a four year rotation of corn, soybeans, corn, and oats with sweetclover (ROT). The corn-beans and four-year rotations have three treatments: conventional use of commercial herbicides and fertilizer (HFCB and HFROT); fertilizer but no herbicides (FOCB and FOROT); and an organic treatment with no commercial herbicides or fertilizer (ORGCB and ORGROT). This last alternative employs manure as a fertility supplement to the soybean rotation.

The crop yields for each of the seven cropping systems were taken from experimental trials done by Sahs and Lesoing (1985; 1990) at the University of Nebraska for the years 1980–89.

The experimental results for each of the seven cropping systems are presented in Table 21. For the four-year rotation, yields were about the same for all systems. Corn and soybean yields are lower under the nonpurchased chemical alternative (ORGROT) than under the other two alternatives. For corn, four-year rotation systems generally give lower yields than do the other systems (both the two-year rotation and the continuous corn). For soybeans,

Table 20. Common Crop Rotations Used on Land Producing Corn, 1988

Previous Crop		Nebraska			10 State Average[a]
1986	1987	State	Dry	Irrigated	
Million Acres Planted					
		6.9	2.3	4.6	53.2
Percent					
Corn	Corn	62	24	79	26
Corn	Soybean	4	6	3	5
Corn	Alfalfa	1	4	nr	3
Corn	Other	3	1	4	3
Soybean	Corn	22	44	8	38
Soybean	Soybean	2	4	1	4
Soybean	Other	nr	1	nr	3
Wheat	Corn	nr	1	nr	1
Wheat	Other	3	6	1	3
Alfalfa	Alfalfa	nr	nr	1	4
Alfalfa	Other	nr	nr	nr	1
Oats	Corn	1	3	nr	1
Oats	Other	1	1	1	1
	Total	99	95	98	94

Source: Daberkow and Gill, 1989, p. 35

nr—none reported

a. The ten states included here are: Illinois, Indiana, Iowa, Michigan, Minnesota, Missouri, Nebraska, Ohio, South Dakota and Wisconsin.

the four-year rotation yields are more comparable to the other alternatives.

Table 22 presents the long-term yield changes for each cropping system. The four-year rotation system with purchased herbicides and fertilizer has erosion rates 16 percent lower than the HF corn-bean treatment. Moreover, the use of manure (ORGCB and ORGROT) rather than purchased fertilizer reduces erosion rates by 16 percent and 41 percent, respectively.

The estimated changes in yields due to erosion amounted to a 7 percent decline over a 30-year period for continuous corn, and a 1 percent decline for the corn-beans treatment using inorganic inputs. For the 4-year organic cropping system, yields increase on average more than 3 percent over the 30-year period.

Physical changes in the soil under different cropping systems have been examined in several studies. Fraser et al. (1988) observed

Table 21. Average Crop Yields from Nebraska Experimental Trials

Rotation	Corn	Soybeans	Oats
Continuous Corn	68	—	—
Corn-Soybeans			
w/Herbicides and Fertilizer Use	90	38	—
w/Fertilizer Use Only	87	37	—
w/Organic Treatment	84	35	—
Corn-Soybeans-Corn-Oats/Clover			
w/Herbicides and Fertilizer Use	84	38	66
w/Fertilizer Use Only	80	37	63
w/Organic Treatment	78	35	61

that microbial populations increased when manure was applied. Sahs and Lesoing (1990) reported on soil characteristics for the Nebraska site in a study of organic matter, phosphorous, potassium, pH, and total nitrogen measured in 1987. These characteristics were examined for ORGROT, HFROT, FOROT, and continuous corn. *(See Table 23)*. For more detail on the four-year rotations, see Sahs and Lesoing (1985).

Estimated Costs

Production costs were estimated for variable inputs including chemicals, direct labor use and user costs of machinery. Indirect and fixed costs of labor, management, and land were not included. All costs were normalized for the 1990 reference year. Basic cost estimates were developed from field records and Jose et al. (1989). The prices for production inputs were assumed to be the same for the different policy scenarios. Under each cropping system, each field operation was charged for its labor use. A fixed cost plus operating costs were charged for each use of a tractor or field machine. For the organic treatment system, manuring costs were charged only for application. Other variable costs included seed, trucking, fuel, repairs, and interest on operating expenses. Charges for spraying and fertilizer application were also included. Labor costs for field operations were

included in the analysis but costs associated with management time were not.

The results of the economic analysis reported here are significantly different from those reported previously by Helmers, Langemeier and Atwood (1986). Some differences arise from the use of a different accounting framework and alternative policy scenarios. The main differences, however, stem from the use of different underlying yield comparisons for conventional and alternative practices. The agronomic data used for the 1986 study were based on two separate experiments on different fields at the University of Nebraska research farm at Mead. One of these experiments focussed primarily on conventional practices, while the other (Sahs and Lesoing, 1986 and 1990) focussed on alternative cropping practices.

For a treatment that both experiments tried—continuous conventional corn at the same level of fertilizer use—the yields differed by as much as 50 percent. This result calls in question the advisability of combining data from the two experiments. For this reason the agronomic data for this report were derived exclusively from the Sahs and Lesoing trials.

To derive agronomic data for the three corn-beans treatments from these experiments, we

Table 22. Yield Estimates for Nebraska Case Study Using the EPIC Model		
Rotation	**Yield** (bushels/acre)	
	Initial	Yr. 30
Continuous Corn	108	101
Corn-Beans		
w/Herbicides & Fertilizer		
corn	137	134
soybeans	39.1	38.1
w/Fertilizer Only		
corn	136	134
soybeans	39.1	38.1
w/Organic Treatment		
corn	90.4	94.1
soybeans	37.6	37.7
Corn-Beans-Corn-Oats/Clover		
w/Herbicides & Fertilizer		
corn	149	150
soybeans	38.5	39.0
oats	34.2	34.8
w/Fertilizer Only		
corn	148	150
soybeans	38.1	38.3
oats	33.8	33.9
w/Organic Treatment		
corn	85.6	91.2
soybeans	38.2	37.8
oats	23.1	24.5

comparisons of alternative treatments, as well as alternative rotations.

Policy Analysis for Nebraska Case Study

Compared with those in Pennsylvania, Nebraska's on-farm and off-farm resource costs are low and including them does not cause a shift in the economic comparison between the three corn-beans and the three four-year corn-beans-corn-oats/clover alternative rotations. The $20 difference in soil depreciation allowances for the herbicides and fertilizer using corn-beans and the organic corn-beans treatments does, however, help to narrow the margin between these treatments to a 2 percent difference in net farm income per acre.

Not surprisingly considering Nebraska's good soils, its soil resource costs are small. In Nebraska as in Pennsylvania, conventional treatments and rotations have higher depreciation and higher erosion rates than alternative rotations and organic treatments—but the differences are less. For the conventional continuous corn rotation the soil depreciation allowance is estimated at 26 percent of the gross operating margin under baseline policy. For the four-year rotation, using green manures and no agrichemicals, soil appreciation amounts to about 4 percent of the gross operating margin; the absolute difference, though, is only about $11 per acre per year.

The omission of resource costs for groundwater contamination, a serious problem in Nebraska, may be important. However, because groundwater models cannot yet reliably represent the impact of various rotations and treatments on the extent of groundwater pollution, these costs remain unknown.

As in Pennsylvania, multilateral decoupling produces the largest net economic value both overall and for each rotation. *(See Figure 8 and Tables 28A and 28B).* Under this policy the herbicides and fertilizer and fertilizer-only corn-beans treatments have the highest net economic value. The organic treatment trails by

used the soybean, and corn after soybean yields from the four-year corn-soybean-corn-oats/clover treatments. This use of the data may overestimate yields for the corn-beans treatments by a small amount due to the rotation effect, but the yield data across rotations and treatments will be more consistent than it would have been had we combined data from two different experiments. This use of the data has the additional advantage of allowing

Table 23. 1987 Soil Data for Nebraska Field Trials

Treatment	Organic Matter (%)	Phosphorous (p.p.m.)	Potassium (p.p.m.)	pH	Total Nitrogen
CC	2.93	20	327	6.38	.161
HFROT	2.99	15	352	6.70	.165
FOROT	2.94	13	327	6.82	.164
ORGROT	3.68	109	564	7.03	.197

CC   – Conventional continuous corn
HFROT   – Corn-soybean-corn-oats/clover w/herbicides and fertilizer
FOROT   – Corn-soybean-corn-oats/clover w/fertilizer but no herbicides
ORGROT – Organic corn-soybean-corn-oats/clover

Table 24. Production Costs and Crop Sales—Nebraska, under Baseline Policy

($/acre/4 years)

Treatment	Total Production Costs	Operating Costs	Fertilizer & Pesticide Costs	Labor Costs	Crop Sales
Continuous Corn	383	209	142	32	502
Corn-Beans					
w/Herbicides & Fertilizer	272	181	65	26	773
w/Fertilizer Only	248	186	29	32	750
w/Organic Treatment	243	207	0	36	716
Corn-Beans-Corn Oats/Clover					
w/Herbicides & Fertilizer	284	185	72	27	634
w/Fertilizer Only	261	185	46	30	609
w/Organic Treatment	253	222	0	32	587

Table 25. Input Price Assumptions,
Nebraska

Hired Labor	$6.00/hour
Anhydrous Ammonia	$0.12/lb. N
0–46–0	$0.25/lb. P_2O_5
Diesel Fuel (less tax)	$0.60/gallon
Interest	5.00%—real

1 percent, only $2 per acre per year. Were groundwater contamination costs included in the analysis, this small difference might be eliminated or reversed. It is fair to say that even in Nebraska, this study finds organic farming to be economically competitive under complete cost accounting.

The four-year rotations produce only about 80 percent of the economic value of the corn-beans rotations, because substituting a year of oats and clover for a second year of soybeans, a more profitable crop, reduces returns.

Under baseline policy, net economic value is lower for each rotation and treatment than under decoupling. The net economic value of the continuous corn rotation commonly followed in Nebraska, for example, is only about 30 percent of its value under the multilateral decoupling scenario. For the other rotations and treatments net economic value is reduced by 15 to 20 percent. Net farm incomes are also lower for all rotations under baseline policy, except for the two corn-beans treatments with herbicides and/or fertilizer.

Net economic values for all rotations and treatments are significantly lower under the Sustainable Agriculture Adjustment Act than under decoupling and slightly less than under the baseline policy scenario, primarily because

of lower predicted crop prices. *(See Figure 8.)* The difference between the corn-beans and four-year rotations is much closer than under baseline policy, but not under multilateral decoupling, largely because four-year rotations receive higher support payments under SAAA. Of the policies tested, only SAAA and multilateral decoupling always provide incentives in line with the underlying resource economics for both Nebraska and Pennsylvania.

The NCA program produces the lowest net economic values for each rotation and treatment in Nebraska. Relative to the decoupling scenario, government payments are higher and net economic value is lower. In Nebraska, where the alternative four-year rotation includes all program crops, the NCA option improves financial and economic comparisons to conventional rotations, relative to the comparisons under baseline policy. In Pennsylvania, however, where the alternative rotations include nonprogram crops, a farmer would be forced to choose between crop sales or program payments on acreage under nonprogram crops. For this reason, the NCA program as recently formulated and represented here, will be less effective than either multilateral decoupling or the SAAA option in removing biases against resource-conserving farming practices.

The 25 percent input tax has a significant impact on the relative profitability of the treatments, but not of the rotations. For the corn-beans treatments, the 25 percent tax makes the herbicides and fertilizer treatment the least profitable. The fertilizer-only treatment is still the most profitable, but the margin between that and the organic treatment is reduced to less than $1 per acre per year. A tax of 11 percent would make the herbicides-fertilizer and organic corn-beans treatments equally profitable.

III. Summary of Policy Conclusions

Several key conclusions can be summarized from the preceding analyses of the Pennsylvania and Nebraska case studies:

1. Farm support mechanisms that transfer income through commodity programs create distortions that encourage dependence on inorganic inputs and discourage sustainable agricultural practices. Baseline agricultural policies reduce the net economic value of all practices compared to multilateral decoupling.

2. A policy of multilateral decoupling, with farm income support provided through means not linked to the commodity programs, could remove the distorting influence of commodity programs and greatly encourage agricultural sustainability, while at the same time reducing fiscal costs.

3. An agrichemical input tax could encourage lower levels of input use, and where economically viable alternatives exist, could cause a shift to alternative agricultural practices.

4. Adaptations to baseline agricultural policy which allow flexibility in crop production could go far towards encouraging sustainable practices. However, net economic value resulting from these alternative policies would most likely be less than that for the multilateral decoupling option.

5. When "conventional" and "alternative" farming systems are evaluated with complete accounting for their on-farm and off-farm environmental costs and without the distorting effects of baseline agricultural policies, farming systems that make maximum use of rotations and biological nutrients are economically competitive even where environmental costs are low, and markedly superior where environmental costs are high.

6. Shifting toward these farming systems through appropriate policy changes can raise agricultural productivity, reduce the fiscal costs of maintaining farm incomes, and lower environmental costs in agriculture. These policy changes can greatly reduce America's farm bill.

Paul Faeth is an Associate in the World Resources Institute's Program in Economics and Technology where he directs WRI's project on the Economics of Sustainable Agriculture. Previously, he worked at the International Institute for Environment and Development and the USDA's Economic Research Service. **Robert Repetto** is Director of the Program in Economics and Technology at the World Resources Institute. Formerly, he was an associate professor of economics in the School of Public Health at Harvard University and a member of the economics faculty at Harvard's Center for Population Studies. **Kim Kroll** is an agricultural systems modeler at the Rodale Research Center. Before joining Rodale's staff in 1987 he was a visiting professor at Rutgers University. **Qi Dai** is a research associate in the Department of Agricultural Economics at Purdue University where he recently completed his Ph.D degree. **Glenn Helmers** is a Professor in the Department of Agricultural Economics at the University of Nebraska.

Table 26A. Summary Results—Pennsylvania—Transition Period Plus Present Value of the Normal Period

Net Economic Value
($/acre/10 years)

	Policy	Conventional Tillage				Reduced Tillage				
		CC	CCBCB	ACG	ACGF	CC	CCBCB	ACG	ACGF	ALL HAY
Gross Operating Margin	Baseline	(47)	607	486	508	(75)	581	480	501	247
	SAAA	(118)	461	461	492	(146)	437	455	485	247
	NCA	(118)	461	235	294	(146)	437	229	287	247
	MLDC	631	959	734	639	603	934	728	632	247
	25% Tax	(168)	523	486	508	(196)	497	480	501	247
– Soil Depreciation	Baseline	231	230	(26)	(78)	228	222	(34)	(95)	(45)
	SAAA	222	215	(24)	(73)	218	207	(32)	(90)	(45)
	NCA	222	215	(24)	(73)	218	207	(32)	(90)	(45)
	MLDC	285	246	(28)	(77)	282	241	(37)	(93)	(45)
	25% Tax	231	230	(26)	(78)	228	222	(34)	(95)	(45)
Net Farm Operating Income	Baseline	(278)	377	512	587	(302)	359	514	596	292
	SAAA	(340)	247	485	565	(364)	230	487	574	292
	NCA	(340)	247	259	367	(364)	230	261	376	292
	MLDC	346	712	762	716	322	694	766	725	292
	25% Tax	(399)	293	512	587	(424)	275	514	596	292
– Off-Site Costs	Baseline	641	438	304	242	494	382	250	183	50
	SAAA	641	438	323	250	494	382	265	190	50
	NCA	641	438	295	231	494	382	244	175	50
	MLDC	705	462	323	250	543	403	265	190	50
	25% Tax	641	438	304	242	494	382	250	183	50
Net Economic Value	Baseline	(919)	(61)	208	345	(796)	(23)	264	413	243
	SAAA	(981)	(191)	162	315	(858)	(152)	222	384	243
	NCA	(981)	(191)	(37)	136	(858)	(152)	17	202	243
	MLDC	(359)	251	438	466	(222)	290	500	536	243
	25% Tax[a]	(919)	(61)	208	345	(796)	(23)	264	413	243

CC   – Conventional Continuous Corn
CCBCB – Conventional Corn-Beans
ACG   – Alternative Cash Grain—Organic corn-barley/soybean-wheat/clover-corn-soybean
ACGF   – Alternative Cash Grain w/Fodder—Organic corn-beans-wheat/clover-clover-corn silage

SAAA – Sustainable Agriculture Adjustment Act
NCA   – Normal Crop Acreage
MLDC – Multilateral Decoupling

a. Columns will not add for the input tax, as the amount of tax has been added back to determine the Net Economic Value.

Table 26B. Summary Results—Pennsylvania—Transition Period Plus Present Value of the Normal Period

Net Farm Income
($/acre/10 years)

	Policy	Conventional Tillage				Reduced Tillage				
		CC	CCBCB	ACG	ACGF	CC	CCBCB	ACG	ACGF	ALL HAY
Gross Operating Margin	Baseline	(47)	607	486	508	(75)	581	480	501	247
	SAAA	(118)	461	461	492	(146)	437	455	485	247
	NCA	(118)	461	235	294	(146)	437	229	287	247
	MLDC	631	959	734	639	603	934	728	632	247
	25% Tax	(168)	523	486	508	(196)	497	480	501	247
− Soil Depreciation	Baseline	231	230	(26)	(78)	228	222	(34)	(95)	(45)
	SAAA	222	215	(24)	(73)	218	207	(32)	(90)	(45)
	NCA	222	215	(24)	(73)	218	207	(32)	(90)	(45)
	MLDC	285	246	(28)	(77)	282	241	(37)	(93)	(45)
	25% Tax	231	230	(26)	(78)	228	222	(34)	(95)	(45)
Net Farm Operating Income	Baseline	(278)	377	512	587	(302)	359	514	596	292
	SAAA	(340)	247	485	565	(364)	230	487	574	292
	NCA	(340)	247	259	367	(364)	230	261	376	292
	MLDC	346	712	762	716	322	694	766	725	292
	25% Tax	(399)	293	512	587	(424)	275	514	596	292
+ Government Commodity Subsidy	Baseline	547	328	315	192	547	328	315	192	0
	SAAA	608	366	407	541	608	366	407	541	0
	NCA	608	366	608	312	608	366	608	312	0
	MLDC	—	—	—	—	—	—	—	—	—
	25% Tax	547	328	315	192	547	328	315	192	0
Net Farm Income	Baseline	269	706	827	779	244	687	829	788	292
	SAAA	268	612	892	1106	245	596	894	1115	292
	NCA	268	612	867	679	244	596	869	688	292
	MLDC	346	712	762	716	322	694	766	725	292
	25% Tax	147	622	827	779	123	603	829	788	292

CC   – Conventional Continuous Corn
CCBCB – Conventional Corn-Beans
ACG   – Alternative Cash Grain—Organic corn-barley/soybean-wheat/clover-corn-soybean
ACGF   – Alternative Cash Grain w/Fodder—Organic corn-beans-wheat/clover-clover-corn silage

SAAA – Sustainable Agriculture Adjustment Act
NCA   – Normal Crop Acreage
MLDC – Multilateral Decoupling

55

Table 27A. Summary Results—Pennsylvania—Transition Period

Net Economic Value
($/acre/5 years)

	Policy	Conventional Tillage				Reduced Tillage				
		CC	CCBCB	ACG	ACGF	CC	CCBCB	ACG	ACGF	ALL HAY
Gross Operating Margin	Baseline	(108)	225	61	92	(123)	212	58	88	54
	SAAA	(143)	154	50	81	(158)	141	47	77	54
	NCA	(143)	154	(70)	(7)	(158)	141	(73)	(11)	54
	MLDC	224	398	168	148	209	385	165	144	54
	25% Tax	(173)	181	61	92	(188)	167	58	88	54
−Soil Depreciation	Baseline	124	123	(14)	(42)	122	119	(18)	(51)	(24)
	SAAA	119	115	(13)	(39)	117	111	(17)	(48)	(24)
	NCA	119	115	(13)	(39)	117	111	(17)	(48)	(24)
	MLDC	153	132	(15)	(41)	151	129	(20)	(50)	(24)
	25% Tax	124	123	(14)	(42)	122	119	(18)	(51)	(24)
Net Farm Operating Income	Baseline	(232)	103	75	134	(245)	93	76	139	78
	SAAA	(262)	39	63	120	(275)	30	64	125	78
	NCA	(262)	39	(57)	32	(275)	30	(56)	37	78
	MLDC	71	266	183	189	58	256	185	194	78
	25% Tax	(297)	58	75	134	(310)	48	76	139	78
−Off-Site Costs	Baseline	343	235	163	129	265	205	134	98	27
	SAAA	343	235	173	134	265	205	142	102	27
	NCA	343	235	158	124	265	205	131	94	27
	MLDC	378	247	173	134	291	216	142	102	27
	25% Tax	343	235	163	129	265	205	134	98	27
Net Economic Value	Baseline	(575)	(132)	(88)	5	(510)	(112)	(58)	41	51
	SAAA	(605)	(196)	(110)	(14)	(540)	(175)	(78)	23	51
	NCA	(605)	(196)	(215)	(92)	(540)	(175)	(187)	(57)	51
	MLDC	(307)	19	10	55	(233)	40	43	92	51
	25% Tax[a]	(575)	(132)	(88)	5	(510)	(112)	(58)	41	51

CC   – Conventional Continuous Corn
CCBCB – Conventional Corn-Beans
ACG   – Alternative Cash Grain—Organic corn-barley/soybean-wheat/clover-corn-soybean
ACGF   – Alternative Cash Grain w/Fodder—Organic corn-beans-wheat/clover-clover-corn silage

SAAA – Sustainable Agriculture Adjustment Act
NCA   – Normal Crop Acreage
MLDC – Multilateral Decoupling

a. Since the tax applied to fertilizers and pesticides is a transfer payment, the value of the tax was added back.

Table 27B. Summary Results—Pennsylvania—Transition Period

Net Farm Income
($/acre/5 years)

	Policy	Conventional Tillage				Reduced Tillage				
		CC	CCBCB	ACG	ACGF	CC	CCBCB	ACG	ACGF	ALL HAY
Gross Operating Margin	Baseline	(108)	226	61	92	(123)	212	58	88	54
	SAAA	(143)	154	50	81	(158)	141	47	77	54
	NCA	(143)	154	(70)	(7)	(158)	141	(73)	(11)	54
	MLDC	224	398	168	148	209	385	165	144	54
	25% Tax	(173)	181	61	92	(188)	167	58	88	54
− Soil Depreciation	Baseline	124	123	(14)	(42)	122	119	(18)	(51)	(24)
	SAAA	119	115	(13)	(39)	117	111	(17)	(48)	(24)
	NCA	119	115	(13)	(39)	117	111	(17)	(48)	(24)
	MLDC	153	132	(15)	(41)	151	129	(20)	(50)	(24)
	25% Tax	124	123	(14)	(42)	122	119	(18)	(51)	(24)
Net Farm Operating Income	Baseline	(232)	103	75	134	(245)	93	76	139	78
	SAAA	(262)	39	63	120	(275)	30	64	125	78
	NCA	(262)	39	(57)	32	(275)	30	(56)	37	78
	MLDC	71	266	183	189	58	256	185	194	78
	25% Tax	(297)	58	75	134	(310)	48	76	139	78
+ Government Commodity Subsidy	Baseline	293	176	182	123	293	176	182	123	0
	SAAA	326	196	218	290	326	196	218	290	0
	NCA	326	196	326	167	326	196	326	167	0
	MLDC	—	—	—	—	—	—	—	—	—
	25% Tax	293	176	182	123	293	176	182	123	0
Net Farm Income	Baseline	61	279	257	257	48	269	258	262	78
	SAAA	64	235	281	410	51	226	282	415	78
	NCA	64	235	269	199	51	226	270	204	78
	MLDC	71	266	183	189	58	256	185	194	78
	25% Tax	(4)	234	257	257	(17)	224	258	262	78

CC   – Conventional Continuous Corn
CCBCB – Conventional Corn-Beans
ACG   – Alternative Cash Grain—Organic corn-barley/soybean-wheat/clover-corn-soybean
ACGF   – Alternative Cash Grain w/Fodder—Organic corn-beans-wheat/clover-clover-corn silage

SAAA – Sustainable Agriculture Adjustment Act
NCA   – Normal Crop Acreage
MLDC – Multilateral Decoupling

Table 28A. Summary Results—Nebraska

Net Economic Value
($/acre/4 years)

	Policy	Rotation						
		CC	HFCB	FOCB	ORGCB	HFROT	FOROT	ORGROT
Gross Operating Margin	Baseline	119	501	503	473	351	348	334
	SAAA	99	445	449	422	341	338	325
	NCA	99	445	449	422	299	298	286
	MLDC	305	583	582	551	461	452	436
	25% Tax	83	485	495	473	332	336	334
− Soil Depreciation	Baseline	31	12	11	(8)	(5)	(4)	(12)
	SAAA	30	11	10	(8)	(5)	(4)	(11)
	NCA	30	11	10	(8)	(5)	(4)	(11)
	MLDC	38	13	12	(10)	(6)	(5)	(15)
	25% Tax	31	12	11	(8)	(5)	(4)	(12)
Net Farm Operating Income	Baseline	88	489	492	482	356	352	346
	SAAA	70	434	439	430	346	342	337
	NCA	70	434	439	430	304	302	297
	MLDC	267	571	570	561	467	457	451
	25% Tax	53	473	485	482	338	340	346
—Off-Site Costs	Baseline	16	9	9	8	8	8	6
	SAAA	16	9	9	8	8	8	6
	NCA	16	9	9	8	8	8	6
	MLDC	17	10	10	8	8	8	6
	25% Tax	16	9	9	8	8	8	6
Net Economic Value	Baseline	72	480	483	474	348	344	340
	SAAA	54	425	430	422	338	334	331
	NCA	54	425	430	422	296	294	292
	MLDC	250	561	561	553	458	449	445
	25% Tax[a]	72	480	483	474	348	344	340

CC   – Conventional continuous corn
HFCB   – Conventional corn-beans, w/herbicides and fertilizer
FOCB   – Corn-beans w/fertilizer but no herbicides
ORGCB   – Organic corn-beans
HFROT   – Corn-beans-corn-oats/clover w/herbicides and fertilizer
FOROT   – Corn-beans-corn-oats/clover w/fertilizer but no herbicides
ORGROT – Organic corn-beans-corn-oats/clover

SAAA   – Sustainable Agriculture Adjustment Act
NCA   – Normal Crop Acreage
MLDC   – Multilateral Decoupling

a. Since the tax applied to fertilizers and pesticides is a transfer payment, the value of the tax was added back.

Table 28B. Summary Results—Nebraska

Net Farm Income
($/acre/4 years)

	Policy	CC	HFCB	FOCB	ORGCB	HFROT	FOROT	ORGROT
					Rotation			
Gross Operating	Baseline	119	501	503	473	351	348	334
Margin	SAAA	99	445	449	422	341	338	325
	NCA	99	445	449	422	299	298	286
	MLDC	305	583	582	551	461	452	436
	25% Tax	83	485	495	473	332	336	334
− Soil Depreciation	Baseline	31	12	11	(8)	(5)	(4)	(12)
	SAAA	30	11	10	(8)	(5)	(4)	(11)
	NCA	30	11	10	(8)	(5)	(4)	(11)
	MLDC	38	13	12	(10)	(6)	(5)	(15)
	25% Tax	31	12	11	(8)	(5)	(4)	(12)
Net Farm Operating	Baseline	88	489	492	482	356	352	346
Income	SAAA	70	434	439	430	346	342	337
	NCA	70	434	439	430	304	302	297
	MLDC	267	571	570	561	467	457	451
	25% Tax	53	473	485	482	338	340	346
+ Government	Baseline	199	100	100	100	100	100	100
Commodity	SAAA	222	111	111	111	185	185	185
Subsidy	NCA	222	111	111	111	222	222	222
	MLDC	–	–	–	–	–	–	–
	25% Tax	199	100	100	100	100	100	100
Net Farm Income	Baseline	287	589	592	581	455	451	445
	SAAA	291	545	550	541	531	527	521
	NCA	291	545	550	541	526	524	519
	MLDC	267	571	570	561	467	457	451
	25% Tax[a]	252	572	584	581	437	440	445

CC   – Conventional continuous corn
HFCB   – Conventional corn-beans, w/herbicides and fertilizer
FOCB   – Corn-beans w/fertilizer but no herbicides
ORGCB   – Organic corn-beans
HFROT   – Corn-beans-corn-oats/clover w/herbicides and fertilizer
FOROT   – Corn-beans-corn-oats/clover w/fertilizer but no herbicides
ORGROT   – Organic corn-beans-corn-oats/clover

SAAA   – Sustainable Agriculture Adjustment Act
NCA   – Normal Crop Acreage
MLDC   – Multilateral Decoupling

a. Columns will not add for the input tax, as the amount of tax has been added back to determine the Net Economic Value.

Appendix

Calculation of Off-Site Costs

The off-site costs reported in Tables 4 and 5 are weighted according to the amount of set-aside acreage,[a] and so do not necessarily equal the erosion rate times the off-site cost per ton of erosion. We assumed that the set-aside acreage would be planted in a cover crop and that its erosion rate would be low, similar to that for All Hay. The calculations for these estimates are shown below. The set-aside acreage used here is the average over the rotation and is a function of the crops in the rotation and the number of seasons the crop occupies in the rotation.

	Soil			All Hay				Erosion		Off-Farm
	[Erosion	×	(1−Set-aside)	+ Erosion	×	Set-aside]	×	Damages	=	Erosion Cost
	(t/ac/yr)		(ac/ac)	(t/ac/yr)		(ac/ac)		($/t)		($/ac/yr)
Pennsylvania										
Continuous Corn	[9.26	×	(1−0.10)	+ (0.66	×	0.10)]	×	8.16	=	69
Corn-Beans (CCBCB)	[6.07	×	(1−0.06)	+ (0.66	×	0.06)]	×	8.16	=	47
Alternative Cash Grain	[4.25	×	(1−0.07)	+ (0.66	×	0.07)]	×	8.16	=	32
ACG w/Fodder	[3.29	×	(1−0.03)	+ (0.66	×	0.03)]	×	8.16	=	26
All Hay	[0.66	×	(1−0.00)	+ (0.66	×	0.00)]	×	8.16	=	5
Nebraska										
Continuous Corn	[6.5	×	(1−0.10)	+ (0.66	×	0.10)]	×	0.67	=	4.0
Corn-Beans (CBCB)	[3.7	×	(1−0.05)	+ (0.66	×	0.05)]	×	0.67	=	2.3
Corn-Beans-Corn- Oats/Clover	[3.1	×	(1−0.0625)	+ (0.66	×	0.0625)]	×	0.67	=	2.0

a. Set aside percentages used were: corn, 10%; wheat, 5%; soybeans, 0%; barley, 10%; and oats, 5%.

61

APPENDIX B

Calculation of Soil Depreciation Allowance

The following formula was used to estimate the soil depreciation allowance (SDA):

$$SDA = [(Y_o - Y_n)/(n/RL)] * P_c * \{[1 - 1/(1 + i)^n]/i\},$$

where

Y_o	is initial yield,
Y_n	is final yield,
RL	is rotation length,
n	is period under consideration,
P_c	is crop price, and
i	is real interest rate.

For rotations that include more than one crop, each crop was weighted according to its acreage in the rotation, and these weighted crop depreciation allowances were added to determine the allowance for the rotation as a whole. When comparing rotations of different lengths, the rotation with the longest period was used to calculate the depreciation allowance for all rotations.

The following example for the Pennsylvania Corn-Bean (CCBCB) rotation will serve to illustrate.

$Y_{o, corn}$	= 141,	(From Table 14, estimated using EPIC)
$Y_{o, soybeans}$	= 55.6,	(From Table 14, estimated using EPIC)
$Y_{n, corn}$	= 121,	(From Table 14, estimated using EPIC)
$Y_{n, soybeans}$	= 45.6,	(From Table 14, estimated using EPIC)
RL	= 5,	defined
n	= 30,	defined
P_{corn}	= 2.05,	(From Table 7, estimated by FAPRI)
$P_{soybean}$	= 5.80,	(From Table 7, estimated by FAPRI)
i	= 0.05.	assumed

SDA_{corn}	=	$[(141 - 121)/(30/5)]$	* 2.05 * $\{[1 - 1/(1+.05)^{30}]/.05\}$	= 105
$SDA_{soybeans}$	=	$[(55.6 - 45.6)/6]$	* 5.80 * $\{15.4\}$	= 149
$SDA_{rotation}$	=	$[SDA_{corn} * 3/RL]$	+ $[SDA_{soybean} * 2/RL]$	
		$[105 * (3/5)]$	+ $[149 * (2/5)]$	= 123
$SDA_{rotation,annual}$	=	$SDA_{rotation}/RL$	= 123/5	= 24.6

Notes

1. Derived from U.S. Department of Commerce (1984–90).

2. However, groundwater pollution problems are serious in Nebraska. Nitrate levels near or above EPA's limit for drinking water have been identified in water supplies of nearly one of five rural communities. Small amounts of the pesticide atrazine have been found in water supplies in the irrigated areas of the Platte River Valley (Aiken, 1990). These costs are not included in the comparisons.

3. See for example: Cacek and Langner, 1986; Dobbs, Leddy, and Smolik, 1988; Domanico, Madden, and Partenheimer, 1986; Goldstein and Young, 1987; Helmers, Langemeier, and Atwood, 1986; Lockeretz et al., 1984.

4. The effect of past erosion on productivity has been demonstrated empirically. For example, in Indiana, Schertz et al. (1989) showed productivity losses of 15 percent and 24 percent for corn and soybeans, for severely eroded soils as compared with slightly eroded soils.

5. For additional information and regional case studies, see also Waddell (1985).

6. For an analysis of a working farm using similar practices, see National Research Council, 1989.

7. Crop yields for 1990 are reported in Figures 12 and 14 but because of their late availability have not been included in the analysis.

8. A conventional financial analysis using the RRC agronomic data set was done by Hanson et al. (1990). They found that for a 750-acre representative farm during the transition period (1981–84), profits were significantly lower for the alternative cash grain rotation than for the conventional rotation. After the transition period (1985–89), the alternative rotation was more profitable.

References

Aiken, J.D. 1990. "Agrichemicals, Ground Water Quality and the 1990 Farm Bill." University of Nebraska Cooperative Extension, June 15.

Alt, K., C.T. Osborn, and D. Colacicco. 1989. *Soil Erosion: What Effect on Agricultural Productivity?* Agriculture Information Bulletin Number 556. Washington, D.C.: Economic Research Service, U.S. Department of Agriculture.

Ambur, Owen D. 1988. "Targeting Farm Aid Toward Efficiency." *Forum for Applied Research and Public Policy*, Summer 1988: 41–48.

American Society of Agricultural Engineers. 1984. *Erosion and Soil Productivity: Proceedings of the National Symposium on Erosion and Soil Productivity.* December 10–11, 1984, New Orleans, La.

Beppler, D.C., M.D. Shaw, and L.D. Hoffman. 1981. *Petroleum Energy Requirements for Pennsylvania Corn Production Systems.* University Park, Pa.: Penn State University.

Berardi, G.M. 1987. "Agricultural Export and Farm Policies: Implications for Soil Loss in the U.S." In *Agricultural Soil Loss: Processes, Policies, and Prospects,* ed. J.M. Harlin and G.M. Berardi. Boulder, Co.: Westview Press.

Blandford, D. 1990. "The Costs of Agricultural Protection and the Difference Free Trade Would Make." In *Agricultural Protectionism in the Industrialized World,* ed. F.H. Sanderson. Washington, D.C.: Resources for the Future.

Bovard, James. 1989. *The Farm Fiasco.* San Francisco, CA: Institute for Contemporary Studies.

Cacek, T. and L.L. Langner. 1986. "The economic implications of organic farming." In, *American Journal of Alternative Agriculture,* Vol. I, No. 1: 25–29.

Carr, A.B., W.H. Meyers, T.T. Phipps, and G.E. Rossmiller. 1988. *Decoupling Farm Programs.* Washington, D.C.: National Center for Food and Agricultural Policy, Resources for the Future.

Clark, E. H., J. A. Haverkamp, and W. Chapman. 1985. *Eroding Soils: The Off-Farm Impacts.* Washington, D.C.: The Conservation Foundation.

Council for Agricultural Science and Technology. 1980a. *Social and Economic Impacts of Restricting Pesticide Use in Agriculture.* Report No. 84. Ames, Iowa: Council for Agricultural Science and Technology.

Council for Agricultural Science and Technology. 1980b. *Organic and Conventional Farming Compared.* Report No. 84. Ames, Iowa: Council for Agricultural Science and Technology.

65

Crosson, Pierre. 1981. *Conservation Tillage and Conventional Tillage: A Comparative Assessment.* Ankeny, Iowa: Soil Conservation Society of America.

Crosson, Pierre. 1985. "National Costs of Erosion on Productivity." In *Erosion Soil Productivity: Proceedings of the National Symposium on Erosion and Soil Productivity*, pp. 254–265, St. Joseph, Michigan: American Society of Agricultural Engineers.

Crosson, Pierre, et al. 1985. "A Framework for Analyzing the Productivity Costs of Soil Erosion in the U.S." In Follett and Stewart ed. *Soil Erosion and Crop Productivity*, pp. 482–502, Madison, Wisconsin: American Society of Agronomy.

Crosson, Pierre. 1986. "Soil Erosion and Policy Issues." In Phipps, Tim T., Pierre R. Crosson, and Kent A. Price, *Agriculture and the Environment: The National Center for Food and Agricultural Policy Annual Policy Review 1986.* Washington, D.C.: Resources for the Future.

Crowder, B.M., et al. 1984. *The Effects of Farm Income on Constraining Soil and Plant Nutrient Losses: An Application of the CREAMS Simulation Model.* Research Bulletin 850. University Park, Pa.: Agricultural Experiment Station, Pennsylvania, Penn State University.

Crutchfield, S. 1988. "Controlling Farm Pollution of Coastal Waters. In *Agricultural Outlook*, May issue. Washington, D.C.: Economic Research Service, USDA.

Culik, M.N., J.C. McAllister, M.C. Palada, and S.L. Rieger. 1983. *The Kutztown Farm Report: A Study of a Low-input Crop/Livestock Farm.* Regenerative Agriculture Library, Technical Bulletin. Kutztown, Pa.: Rodale Research Center.

Dabbert, S. and P. Madden. 1986. "The Transition to Organic Agriculture: A Multi-year Model of a Pennsylvania Farm." *American Journal of Alternative Agriculture*, Vol. 1, No. 3: 99–107.

Daberkow, S. and M. Gill. 1989. "Common Crop Rotations Among Major Field Crops." In, *Agricultural Resources: Inputs Situation and Outlook Report.* Report No. AR–15. Washington, D.C.: Economic Research Service, U.S. Department of Agriculture.

Daberkow, S.G. and K.H. Reichelderfer. 1988. "Low-Input Agriculture: Trends, Goals, and Prospects of Input Use." *American Journal of Agricultural Economics*, Vol. 70, No. 5: 1159–1166.

Devadoss, S., et al. 1989. *The FAPRI Modeling System at CARD: A Documentation Summary.* Technical Report 89–TR 13. Ames, Iowa: Center for Agricultural and Rural Development, Iowa State University.

Dobbs, T.L., M.G. Leddy, and J.D. Smolik. 1988. "Factors influencing the economic potential for alternative farming systems: Case analyses in South Dakota." In, *American Journal of Alternative Agriculture*, Vol. 3, No. 1: 26–34.

Domanico, J.L., P. Madden, and E.J. Partenheimer. 1986. "Income effects of limiting soil erosion under organic, conventional and no-till systems in eastern Pennsylvania." *American Journal of Alternative Agriculture*, Vol. 1, No. 2: 75–82.

Dum, S.A., F.A. Hughes, J.G. Cooper, B.W. Kelly and V.E. Crowley. 1981. *Farm Management Handbook.* University Park, Pennsylvania: College of Agriculture, Penn State University.

Dyke, P.T. and E.O. Heady. 1985. "Assessment of Soil Erosion and Crop Productivity with Economic Models." In *Soil Erosion and Crop Productivity*, ed. Follett and Stewart, pp. 105–117, Madison, Wisconsin: American Society of Agronomy.

Edwards, E.O. and P.W. Bell. 1961. *The Theory and Measurement of Business Income.* Berkeley: University of California Press.

Follett, R.F. and B.A. Stewart. 1985. *Soil Erosion and Crop Productivity*. Madison, Wisconsin: American Society of Agronomy.

Food and Agricultural Policy Research Institute (FAPRI). 1988. *Policy Scenarios with the FAPRI Commodity Models*. Working Paper 88–WP 41. Ames, Iowa: Center for Agricultural and Rural Development, Iowa State University.

FAPRI. 1990a. *Draft Report: An Evaluation of Price Support Equilibration Options for the 1990 Farm Bill*. Ames, Iowa: Center for Agricultural and Rural Development, Iowa State University.

FAPRI. 1990b. *FAPRI U.S. Agricultural Outlook*. 1990 Spring Agribusiness Outlook and Policy Conference. Des Moines, Iowa.

Fraser, D.G., J.W. Doran, W.W. Sahs, and G.W. Lesoing. "Soil Microbial Populations and Activities Under Conventional and Organic Management." *Journal of Environmental Quality*, Vol. 17 (1988): 585–590.

Frye, Wilbur W. 1987. "The Effects of Soil Erosion on Crop Productivity." In *Agricultural Soil Loss: Processes, Policies, and Prospects*, ed. J.M. Harlin and G.M. Berardi. Boulder, Co.: Westview Press.

Gardner, B.L. 1987. *The Economics of Agricultural Policies*. New York: Macmillan.

Goldstein, W.A. and D.C. Young. 1987. "An Agronomic and Economic Comparison of a Conventional and a Low-input Cropping System in the Palouse." *American Journal of Alternative Agriculture*, Vol. 2, No. 2: 51–56.

Hallberg, G.R. 1989. "Pesticide Pollution of Groundwater in the Humid United States." *Agriculture, Ecosystems and Environment*, Vol. 26: 299–367.

Hanson, James C., Dale M. Johnson, Steven E. Peters, and Rhonda R. Janke. 1990. *The Profitability of Sustainable Agriculture in the Mid-Atlantic Region: A Case Study Between 1981 and 1989*. Working Paper No. 90–12. College Park, Md.: Department of Agricultural and Resource Economics, University of Maryland.

Harwood, J.L. and C.E. Young. 1989. *Wheat: Background for 1990 Farm Legislation*. U.S. Department of Agriculture, Economic Research Service, Commodity Economics Division, Staff Report No. AGES 89-56. Washington, D.C.

Hayami, Y., and V. Ruttan. 1985. *Agricultural Development: An International Perspective*. Baltimore: Johns Hopkins University Press.

Heady, E.O. 1948. "The Economics of Rotations with Farm and Production Policy Applications." *Journal of Farm Economics*, Vol. 30, No. 4: 645–664.

Heimlich, R.E. 1989. *Productivity and Erodibility of U.S. Cropland*. Agricultural Economic Report Number 604. Washington, D.C.: Economic Research Service, U.S. Department of Agriculture.

Helmers, G.A., M.R. Langemeier, and J. Atwood. 1986. "An Economic Analysis of Alternative Cropping Systems for East-central Nebraska." *American Journal of Alternative Agriculture*, Vol. 1, No. 4: 153–158.

Hicks, John R. 1946. *Value and Capital: An Inquiry into Some Fundamental Principles of Economic Theory*. Oxford: Oxford University Press.

Hrubovcak, J., M. LeBlanc, and J. Miranowski. 1990. "Limitations in Evaluating Environmental and Agrichemical Policy Coordination Benefits." In, *AEA Papers and Proceedings: Environmental and Agricultural Policies*, Vol. 80, No. 2: 208–212.

Jose, H.D., et al. 1989. *Estimated Crop and Livestock Production Costs—1989*. Nebraska Cooperative Extension EC–872.

Kahn, J.R. 1987. "Economic damage from herbicide pollution in Chesapeake Bay." *Project Appraisal*, Vol. 2, No. 3: 142–152.

Larson, W.E., F.J. Pierce, and R.H. Dowdy. 1983. "The Threat of Soil Erosion to Long-term Crop Production." *Science*, Vol. 219: 458–465.

Larson, W.E., et al. 1985. "Effects of Soil Erosion on Soil Properties as Related to Crop Productivity and Classification." In *Soil Erosion and Crop Productivity*, ed. Follett and Stewart, pp. 190–210, Madison, Wisconsin: American Society of Agronomy.

Lockeretz, W., G. Shearer, D.H. Kohl, and R.W. Klepper. 1984. "Comparison of Organic and Conventional Farming in the Corn Belt." In, *Organic Farming: Current Technology and Its Role in a Sustainable Agriculture*. Madison, Wisconsin: American Society of Agronomy.

Lowrance, R., P.F. Hendrix, and E.P. Odum. 1986. "A hierarchical approach to sustainable agriculture." *American Journal of Alternative Agriculture*, Vol. 1, No. 4: 169–173.

Mercier, S. 1989. *Corn: Background for 1990 Farm Legislation*. U.S. Department of Agriculture, Economic Research Service, Commodity Economics Division, Staff Report No. AGES 89–47. Washington, D.C.

Meyer, L.D., et al. 1985. "Experimental Approaches for Quantifying the Effect of Soil Erosion on Productivity." In *Soil Erosion and Crop Productivity*, ed. Follett and Stewart, pp. 214–232, Madison, Wisconsin: American Society of Agronomy.

National Erosion-Soil Productivity Research Committee. 1981. "Soil Erosion Effects on Soil Productivity: A Research Perspective." *Journal of Soil and Water Conservation*, Vol. 36: 82–90.

National Research Council. 1989. *Alternative Agriculture*. Washington, D.C.: National Academy Press.

Nielsen, E.G. and L.K. Lee. 1987. *The Magnitude and Costs of Groundwater Contamination From Agricultural Chemicals: A National Perspective*. U.S. Department of Agriculture, Economic Research Service, Agricultural Economic Report Number 576, Washington, D.C.

O'Connell, P. 1990. Briefing Materials on Sustainable Agriculture Activities in USDA. Not published. Cooperative State Research Service, U.S. Department of Agriculture.

Penn State Agricultural Extension Service. 1987. *Penn State Agronomy Guide*. University Park, Pa.: Penn State University.

Phipps, T.T. and K. Reichelderfer. 1988. *Agricultural Policy and Environmental Quality*. Washington, D.C.: Resources for the Future.

Phipps, T.T. and K. Reichelderfer. 1989. "Farm support and environmental quality at odds?" *Resources*, Spring: 14–15.

Pierce, F.J., W.E. Larson, R.H. Dowdy, and W. Graham. 1983. "Productivity of Soils: Assessing long-term change due to erosion." *Journal of Soil and Water Conservation*, Vol. 38: 39–44.

Pimentel, David. 1987. "Soil Erosion Effects on Farm Income." In *Agricultural Soil Loss: Processes, Policies, and Prospects*, ed. J.M. Harlin and G.M. Berardi. Boulder, Co.: Westview Press.

Reid, W.S. 1985. "Regional Effects of Soil Erosion on Crop Productivity." In Follett and Stewart ed. *Soil Erosion and Crop Productivity*, pp. 235–249, Madison, Wisconsin: American Society of Agronomy.

Repetto, R., W. Magrath, M. Wells, C. Beer, and F. Rossini. 1989. *Wasting Assets: Natural Resources in the National Income Accounts*. Washington, D.C.: World Resources Institute.

Ribaudo, Marc O. 1989. *Water Quality Benefits from the Conservation Reserve Program*. U.S.

Department of Agriculture, Resources and Technology Division, Economic Research Service. Agricultural Economic Report No. 606. February 1989. Ribaudo, Marc. Personal interview. July 10, 1990. U.S. Department of Agriculture, Economic Research Service, Washington, D.C.

Runge, C. Ford. 1986. "Induced Innovation in Agriculture and Environmental Quality." In Phipps, Crosson, and Price ed. *Agriculture and the Environment*. Washington, D.C.: Resources for the Future.

Runge, C.F., R.D. Munson, E. Lotterman and J. Creason. 1990. *Agricultural Competitiveness, Farm Fertilizer and Chemical Use, and Environmental Quality: A Descriptive Analysis*. St. Paul, Minnesota: Center for International Food and Agricultural Policy, University of Minnesota.

Sahs, W.W. and G. Lesoing. 1985. "Crop Rotations and Manure Versus Agricultural Chemicals in Dryland Grain Production." *Journal of Soil and Water Conservation*, Vol. 40: 511–516.

Sahs, W.W. and G. Lesoing. Progress Report, University of Nebraska Agricultural Research Project 12–58, Jan. 25, 1990.

Schaffer, J.D. and G.W. Whittaker. "Average Farm Incomes: They're Highest Among Farmers Receiving the Largest Direct Government Payments." *Choices*, Second Quarter, 1990, 30–31.

Schertz, D.L., W.C. Moldenhauer, S.J. Livingston, G.A. Weesies, and E.A. Hintz. "Effect of past soil erosion on crop productivity in Indiana." In, *Journal of Soil and Water Conservation*, November–December 1989: 604–608.

Shrader, W.O. and R.D. Voss. 1980. "Soil Fertility: Crop Rotation vs. Monoculture." *Crop and Soil Magazine*, Vol. 7: 15–18.

Smith, R.A., R.B. Alexander, and M.G. Wolman. 1987. "Water-Quality Trends in the Nation's Rivers." *Science*, Vol. 235: 1607–1615.

Tammen, Ronald L. Personal interview. July 27, 1990. Organic Foods Alliance, Arlington, Virginia.

Taylor, C.R. and K.K. Frohberg. 1977. "The Welfare Effects of Erosion Controls, Banning Pesticides, and Limiting Fertilizer in the Corn Belt." *American Journal of Agricultural Economics*, Vol. 59: 25–36.

U.S. Department of Agriculture. 1980. Study Team on Organic Farming. Report and Recommendations on Organic Farming. Washington, D.C.

U.S. Department of Agriculture, 1989. *1989 Agricultural Chartbook*. Agriculture Handbook No. 684. Washington, D.C.: Economic Research Service.

U.S. Department of Agriculture. 1990. *1990 Farm Bill: Proposal of the Administration*. Washington, D.C.: Office of Publishing and Visual Communications, February 1990.

U.S. Department of Commerce. 1984–1990. *Statistical Abstracts of the United States*. Washington, D.C.: U.S. Government Printing Office.

U.S. General Accounting Office. 1990. *Alternative Agriculture: Federal Incentives and Farmers' Opinions*. GAO/PEMD-90-12. Washington, D.C.

U.S. House of Representatives. 1989. Sustainable Agricultural Adjustment Act of 1989, H.R. 3552. 101st Congress, 1st Session.

U.S. House of Representatives. 1990. Food, Agriculture, Conservation, and Trade Act of 1990. Report 101–916. 101st Congress, 2d Session.

Waddell, Thomas E., ed. 1985. The Off-Site Costs of Soil Erosion: Proceedings of a Symposium Held in May 1985. Washington, D.C.: The Conservation Foundation.

Walker, D.J. and D.L. Young. 1986. "Assessing Soil Erosion Productivity Damage." In, *Soil Conservation: Assessing the National Resources*

Inventory, Vol. II.: 21–62. Washington, D.C.: National Academy Press.

Williams, J.R., et al. 1981. "Soil erosion effects on soil productivity: A research perspective." *Journal of Soil and Water Conservation*, Vol. 36, No. 2: 82–90.

Williams, J.R., P.T. Dyke, and C.A. Jones. 1982. "EPIC—A model for assessing the effects of erosion on soil productivity." Proceedings of the Third International Conference on State-of-art in Ecological Modelling. Colorado State University, Fort Collins, Co.

Williams, J.R. and K.G. Renard. 1985. "Assessments of Soil Erosion and Crop Productivity with Process Model (EPIC)." In *Soil Erosion and Crop Productivity*, ed. Follett and Stewart, pp. 68–102, Madison, Wisconsin: American Society of Agronomy.

Williams, J.R., et al. 1989. *EPIC—Erosion/Productivity Impact Calculator: 2, User Manual*. A.N. Sharpley and J.R. Williams, eds. U.S. Department of Agriculture Technical Bulletin No. 1768.

World Resources Institute

1709 New York Avenue, N.W.
Washington, D.C. 20006, U.S.A.

The World Resources Institute (WRI) is a policy research center created in late 1982 to help governments, international organizations, and private business address a fundamental question: How can societies meet basic human needs and nurture economic growth without undermining the natural resources and environmental integrity on which life, economic vitality, and international security depend?

Two dominant concerns influence WRI's choice of projects and other activities:

The destructive effects of poor resource management on economic development and the alleviation of poverty in developing countries; and

The new generation of globally important environmental and resource problems that threaten the economic and environmental interests of the United States and other industrial countries and that have not been addressed with authority in their laws.

The Institute's current areas of policy research include tropical forests, biological diversity, sustainable agriculture, energy, climate change, atmospheric pollution, economic incentives for sustainable development, and resource and environmental information.

WRI's research is aimed at providing accurate information about global resources and population, identifying emerging issues, and developing politically and economically workable proposals.

In developing countries, WRI provides field services and technical program support for governments and non-governmental organizations trying to manage natural resources sustainably.

WRI's work is carried out by an interdisciplinary staff of scientists and experts augmented by a network of formal advisors, collaborators, and cooperating institutions in 50 countries.

WRI is funded by private foundations, United Nations and governmental agencies, corporations, and concerned individuals.